Shipwrecks of the Dominican Republic

and

A Guide to Shipwreck Identification Through Recovered Artifacts

Black Duck
&
Robert Splash Klein

Shipwrecks of the Dominican Republic
and
A Guide to Shipwreck Identification through Recovered Artifacts

by
Black Duck & Robert Splash Klein

Copyright © 2010 Black Duck & Robert Splash Klein
ISBN 978-0-9829477-0-8

PUBLISHING HISTORY
First Edition – August 2010

Printed in the United States of America.
Never Mind Publishing
Contact publisher at: info@nevermindpublishing.com

THE TREASURE FINDER

To be a true treasure finder you must first choose to make this your lifestyle not a hobby or job, but a lifestyle. Unless you are going to self-fund your project, your investors will expect and deserve nothing less from you and your crew. The following quote from the Robin Moore and Howard Jennings book *The Treasure Hunter* basically says it all.

> *"To be a treasure hunter, you have only to want to be a treasure hunter. The rest-the skills, the luck, the adventures, the discoveries, and, yes, the disappointments-will follow in due course. But first you must choose. If you think you would like to be a treasure hunter but aren't sure your wife would approve, or doubt that you could afford to take so long away from your job, or are afraid that, as a woman, you might be compromising your femininity, then in effect you have already made your choice. Because treasure hunting isn't so much a vocation as it is a lifestyle. It isn't enough just to want treasure, or even to want to hunt for treasure. You have to want all the things that go along with treasure hunting: utter freedom, a certain rootlessness, a willingness to take great risks, a readiness to stretch your capacities to their limits, an acceptance of self-discipline, and much, much more. If your primary motive in wanting to be a treasure hunter is to get rich, you are better advised to go to work for a large corporation."*

From: *The Treasure Hunter*
By: Robin Moore and Howard Jennings
Used with permission from the publisher.

DEDICATION

This book is dedicated to:

My esposa and her mother; for without their understanding and support this book would not be possible

My daughter; from whom I have been away for much longer than I ever wanted

All those people who helped me make this book a true treasure

All the treasure hunters who understand that the gold, silver, and jewels are not the true treasures of this business, and who continue to go about the work in a correct, honest, and professional manner.

Also to all the Archeologists who understand and accept the need for salvage/rescue companies that work professionally and correctly – we understand your disappointment and frustration with the treasure hunters who just do not get it.

el
BLACK DUCK

My wife for trusting me and putting up with my long absences

ROBERT SPLASH KLEIN

And a special thanks to the Oficina Nacional de Patrimonio Cultural Subacuatico

FOREWARD

This book is the product of our research, personal experiences, consultations with experts, and thousands of dives looking for shipwrecks. It is not meant to be the answer to everything, and it may be missing important information. It is basically a work-in-progress, and we invite all to give us feedback, new information, corrections, or additions. Our intent is to provide, for both the novice and the experienced treasure hunter, a single reference source for information about the artifacts found on shipwrecks and how they can be used to help determine the age, origin, destination, etc. of the ship. We found many widely accepted assumptions to be incorrect, according to our extensive research. Some subjects in this book are just covered superficially, since entire books have been written on them. We provide extensive references in our "Sources" chapter at the end. We have tried to focus on the history and those items that will help identify shipwrecks. We are not perfect and make mistakes, but we have done our research. We found there are often differing opinions and confusing/conflicting information. We sincerely hope our work helps you in your quest.

The "Shipwrecks of the Dominican Republic" chapter of this book contains factual information about the shipwrecks listed. If the coordinates of the shipwreck are listed, it indicates the wreck was either discovered by the authors, or it was previously known and they have personally dived on it to confirm its existence and location. We are providing the actual coordinates and photos of the wrecks along with some useful information about each site.

Good Hunting!
The authors

BLACK DUCK & ROBERT SPLASH KLEIN

******

CONTENTS

SHIPWRECKS OF THE DOMINICAN REPUBLIC

PEDERNALES/CABO ROJO AREA

This area has some of the most beautiful beaches on the island. It is next to the Haiti border and there is nothing much there. Pedernales is a pretty small town with several small nice hotels. You can hire a boat there for around 100 dollars a day and you pay for fuel.

Beach area near Pedernales at location called Cuevas de las Águilas

Cave Diving

There are some interesting underwater caves to dive in the Pedernales area, but you will need a guide and you should be an advanced cave diver to tackle these caves.

Contacts for cave diving and cave diving rescues or emergencies are:
- Dominican Republic Speleological Society – info@dr-ss.com
- Phillip Lehman – email: philliplehman@mac.com
- Thomas Riffaud – email: thomasrfd@yahoo.fr
- Bobby Pritchett – email: bpb1313@gmail.com
- Dennie Borrett /Golden Arrow Dive Shop –denis@cavediving.com.do

Aerial shot showing three underwater caves near the Pedernales area

The Airplane Wing

Depth: 40 feet or less

Bottom: Hard bottom with sandy pockets

Location: 17° 58.300'N - 71° 43.358'W

Comments: Full wing from a small air plane. It is an easy dive. Watch out for Lion Fish - POISONOUS!

Thomas inspecting The Airplane Wing

Lionfish infestation on The Airplane Wing

Debris Pile:

Depth: Less than 30 feet

Bottom: Hard bottom with sandy pockets

Location: 17° 47.895'N 71° 39.531'W

Comments: This area has some debris that could be from a shipwreck. Also in July of 2010 many Lion Fish – CAREFUL - POISONOUS!

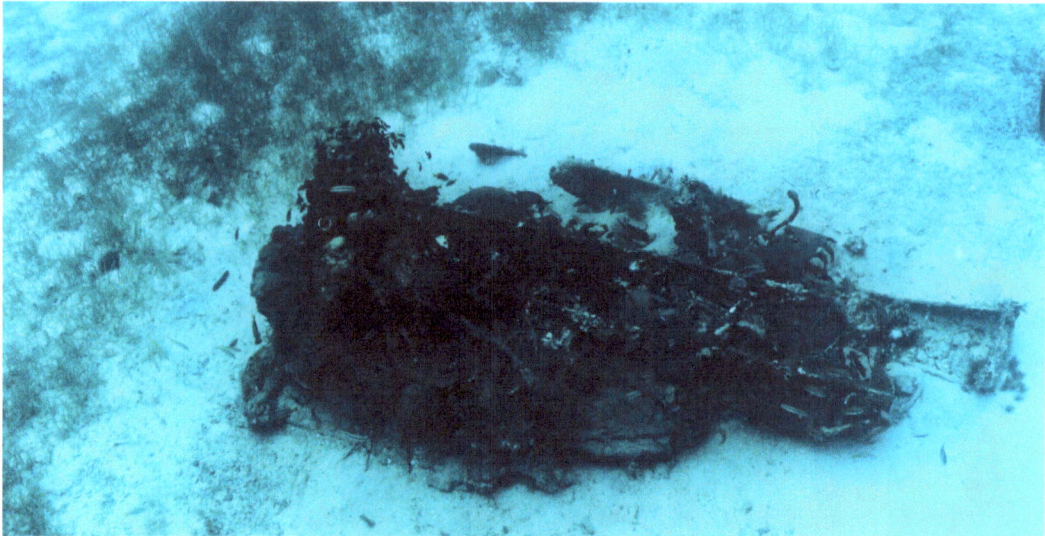

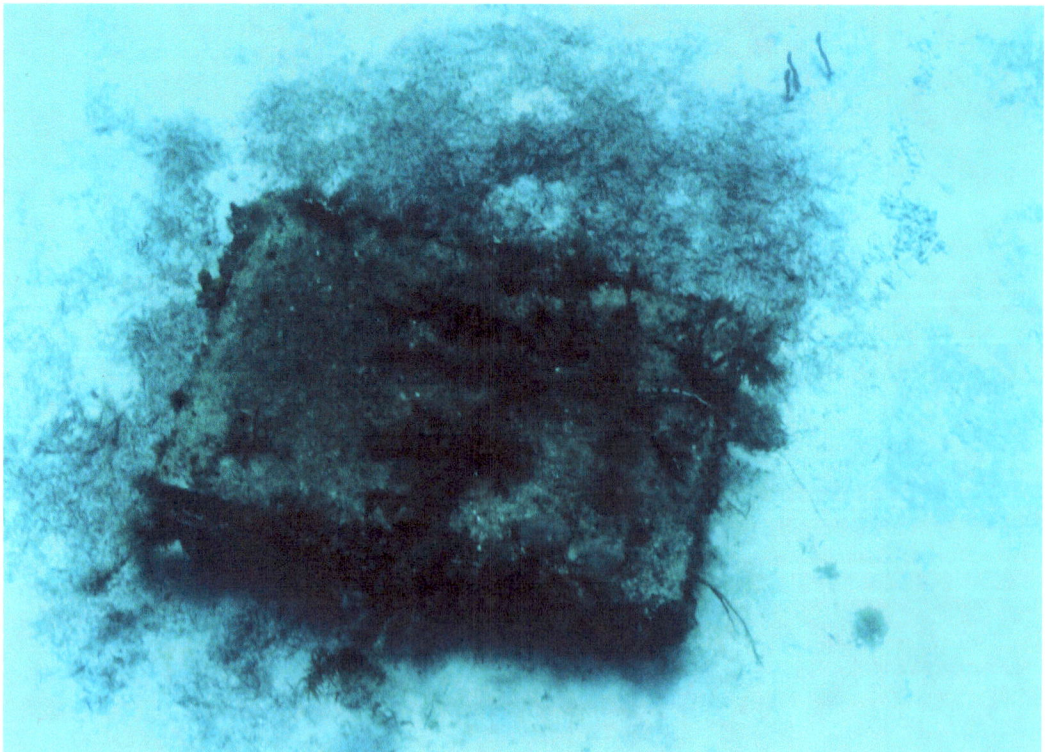

Airplane Engine
Depth: 40 feet or less – easy dive.
Bottom: Hard bottom with sandy pockets
Location: 17° 58.473'N 71° 43.419'W
Comments: Only the engine rests here inside a roll cage.

Anchor without shank
Depth: 40 feet or less – easy dive
Bottom: Hard bottom with sandy pockets
Location: 17° 56.499'N 71° 42.380'W
Comments: This is the first anchor I have seen with out a shank. Maybe a ship was at anchor and the shank broke off leaving arms and palms.

Los Frailes
Los Frailes is a rocky outcropping off the SW of the Dominican Republic where local spear fishermen have reported seeing cannon. This is also one of the favorite dive destinations for sports divers, very pristine and beautiful.

Los Frailes

ISLA BEATA to BARAHONA AREA

The Mast Wreck
Depth: Less than 30 feet
Bottom: Hard bottom with sandy pockets
Location: Near Cabo Mongo
Comments: Mast is sticking out of the water and visible from boat at both high and low tide.

Unknown wreck
Depth: Visible on the reef
Location: 17° 35.817'N 71° 29.552'W
Comments: 200 foot long freighter on reef – north shore of Isla Beata

****

Note: We have found and documented 80 sites with exact GPS coordinates that are not in this book or any other book. These sites are under investigation, and at this time are restricted

Bahoruco Beach Wreck

Depth: Less than 30 feet

Bottom: Hard bottom with sandy pockets

Location: 18° 04. 327 N 71° 05. 357 W

Comments: This dive you can do from shore when the surf is down. Metal ship broken up, engines are still there. Partially exposed at low tide.

Shipwreck visible as a dot in the space between the palm trees

Close-up of the exposed part of the shipwreck

4 Cannon in Bahia de Neiba
Depth: (restricted)
Location: (restricted)

Anchor in Bahia de Neiba
Depth: Less than 40 feet
Bottom: Reef area
Location: 18° 13.056'N 71° 04.013'W
Comments: Access to this location is near the Hotel Larimar

Unknown shipwreck – tugboat near Barahona
Depth: Grounded near beach.
Location: Barahona

DID YOU KNOW?
- Bronze spikes can not ID a time nor country of origin of a Shipwreck. Ship builders used round and square bronze spikes and nails from the Roman days until the 19th century.

Unknown shipwreck

Depth: Less than 30 feet
Bottom: Rocky area
Location: 17° 59.744'N 71° 9.357'W
Comments: Located near Paraiso

Shipwreck near Paraiso – photo by Kevin James

Same shipwreck near Paraiso – taken during aerial survey – courtesy Bobby Pritchett

The St. Joe

Depth: High and dry on the beach

Location: 17° 40.261'N 71° 22.611'W

Comments: Modern wreck on the beach near Cabo Mongo.

Unknown wreck near *The St. Joe*

Depth: Stranded high on the reef.

Location: 17° 40.526'N 71° 22.319'W

Comments: Near to St. Joe site – near Cabo Mongo

Anchors from unknown wrecks in Barahona area

The following photos show anchors that were recovered by local fishermen and placed on display at various locations in Barahona.

PUERTO VIEJO AREA

Unknown wreck

Depth: Less than 30 feet – partially visible at low tide

Location: Near Puerto Viejo

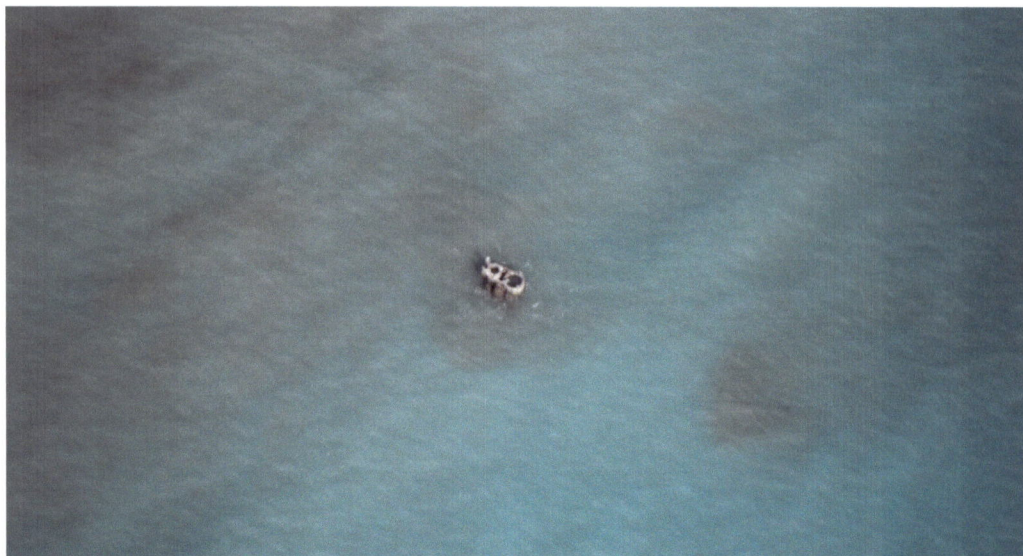

DID YOU KNOW?

- Just because it said there were 74 cannon on a ship doesn't make it true. When a ship was leaving port it was required to have a certain number of cannon onboard depending on its tonnage. If they did not have enough cannon, they would make wooden ones and paint them black, then pay off the inspector and leave port. There are also documented cases where cannon were left behind to make room for more contraband – a very lucrative side business for the captain of the ship.

AZUA/OCOA BAY AREA

Ocoa bay is a great place for boating. Almost every day until 11:AM the water is completely flat. There are three hotels on the Bay. In Las Salinas there is the **Salinas Hotel**, George Dominic is the owner. Then there is a small hotel In Palmar de Ocoa. My favorite of the three is **Hotel Playa Mia** in Hatillo/Azua with great sunsets, excellent food, and one of the most tranquil places to stay on the Island.

The five Cannon Shipwreck

Depth: 25 feet or less
Bottom: Hard bottom with sand pockets and some reef area
Location: NW side of Ocoa Bay (exact location restricted)
Comments: In 2003 an older retired fisherman called Rubin showed the author this wreck, consisting of five cannon (hence the name) and an old wooden hull. The hull has a copper bottom and is totally encrusted in the coral. It lies in 6 - 12 feet of water. It is close to shore and conditions are very rough at times.

Puerto Tortuguero
Unknown wreck ("Ballast Wreck")

Depth: 25 feet or less

Bottom: Very silty, sandy, muddy area, but can be very clear at times.

Location: 18° 25.591'N 70° 41.435'W

Comments: In Ocoa Bay You can drive right up to it. The author discovered this wreck while doing aerial surveys in 2009. We spotted this ballast pile and another more modern wreck a few hundred yards away. This wreck is about 50 yards from shore. It should be noted that this site is right in front of the Marine outpost and any attempt to salvage any shipwreck could result in incarceration and serious legal issues.

Ballast pile seen from the air

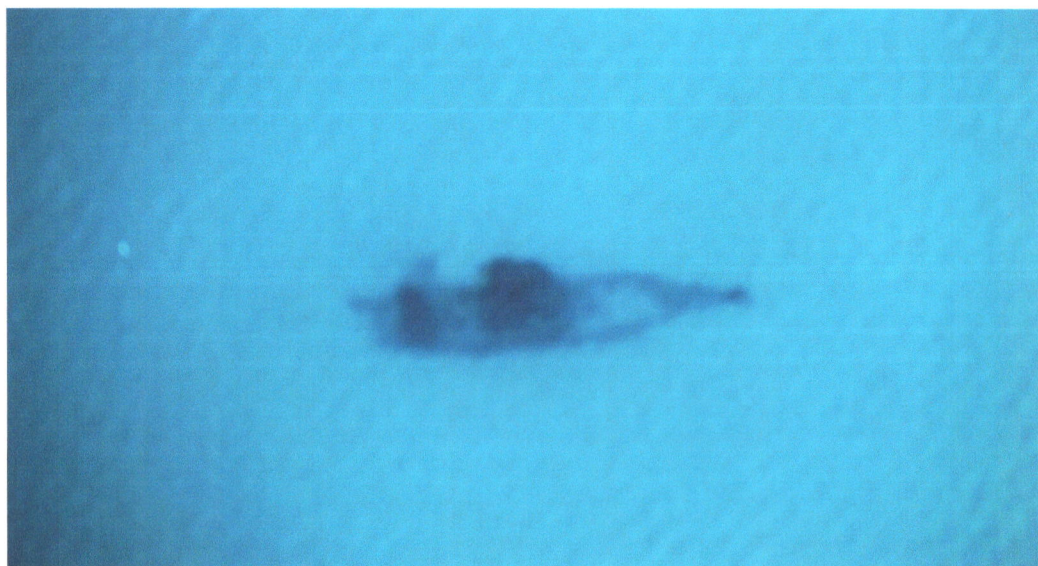

Modern shipwreck seen from the air NW area of Ocoa Bay

The Phoenix – also known as "The Cocaine Wreck"

Depth: 130 feet max depth - average depth 75 feet
Bottom: Hard Bottom
Location: Ocoa bay 18° 13.682'N 70° 33.724'W
Comments: Locally referred to as the "Cocaine Wreck" because it was seized by the Dominican Navy while transporting cocaine. It was purposely scuttled after stripping most things of value. The ship is approximately 250 feet long and 45 feet wide

Anchor in el Gran Segovia Restaurant in Azua

Comments: The author was told this anchor came from an unknown shipwreck in Ocoa Bay.

Unknown Wreck

Depth: Less than 30 feet
Location: Visible from the beach near Matanzas

SANTO DOMINGO/PALENQUE

The *Impérial* and *Diomède*

Depth: less than 30 feet
Bottom: Hard bottom with sand pockets
Location: Near Palenque (exact location restricted)
Comments: The Battle of San Domingo, in 1806, was a naval battle of the Napoleonic Wars. French and British squadrons of ships of the line met off the southern coast of the French-occupied Spanish Colony of Santo Domingo (usually written as San Domingo in contemporary British usage) in the Caribbean. The French squadron, under Vice-Admiral Corentin Urbain Leissègues in the 120-gun *Impérial*, had sailed from Brest in December 1805, one of two squadrons intending to raid British trade routes as part of the Atlantic campaign of 1806.

Separating from the squadron under Contre-Admiral Jean-Baptiste Willaumez in the mid-Atlantic, Leissègues sailed for the Caribbean. After winter storms near the Azores damaged and scattered his squadron, Leissègues regrouped and repaired his ships at the city of Santo Domingo, where a British squadron under Vice-Admiral Sir John Thomas Duckworth discovered them on 6 February 1806. Duckworth had abandoned his assigned station off Cadiz in pursuit of Willaumez during December and traveled so far across the Atlantic in pursuit that he was forced to resupply at St. Kitts in the Leeward Islands, where news had reached him of Leissègues' arrival.

By the time French lookouts at Santo Domingo had spotted Duckworth approaching from the southeast, it was too late for Leissègues to escape. Sailing with the wind westwards along the coast, Leissègues formed a line of battle to meet the approaching British squadron, which had split into two divisions. Although his divisions separated during the approach, Duckworth's lead ships remained in a tight formation and successfully engaged the head of the French line, targeting the flagship *Impérial*. Under pressure, the French squadron broke apart, the British isolating and capturing three ships before concentrating on the main combat around the French flagship. Severely damaged and surrounded, Leissègues drove *Impérial* ashore to avoid capture. The remaining French ship of the line, *Diomède*, followed him. Although most of the crew of these ships scrambled ashore, British boarding parties captured both vessels and set them on fire.

The following maps are very rare maps showing the route the ships took trying to escape the British and then the final battle where the Imperial and Diomede finally met their doom.

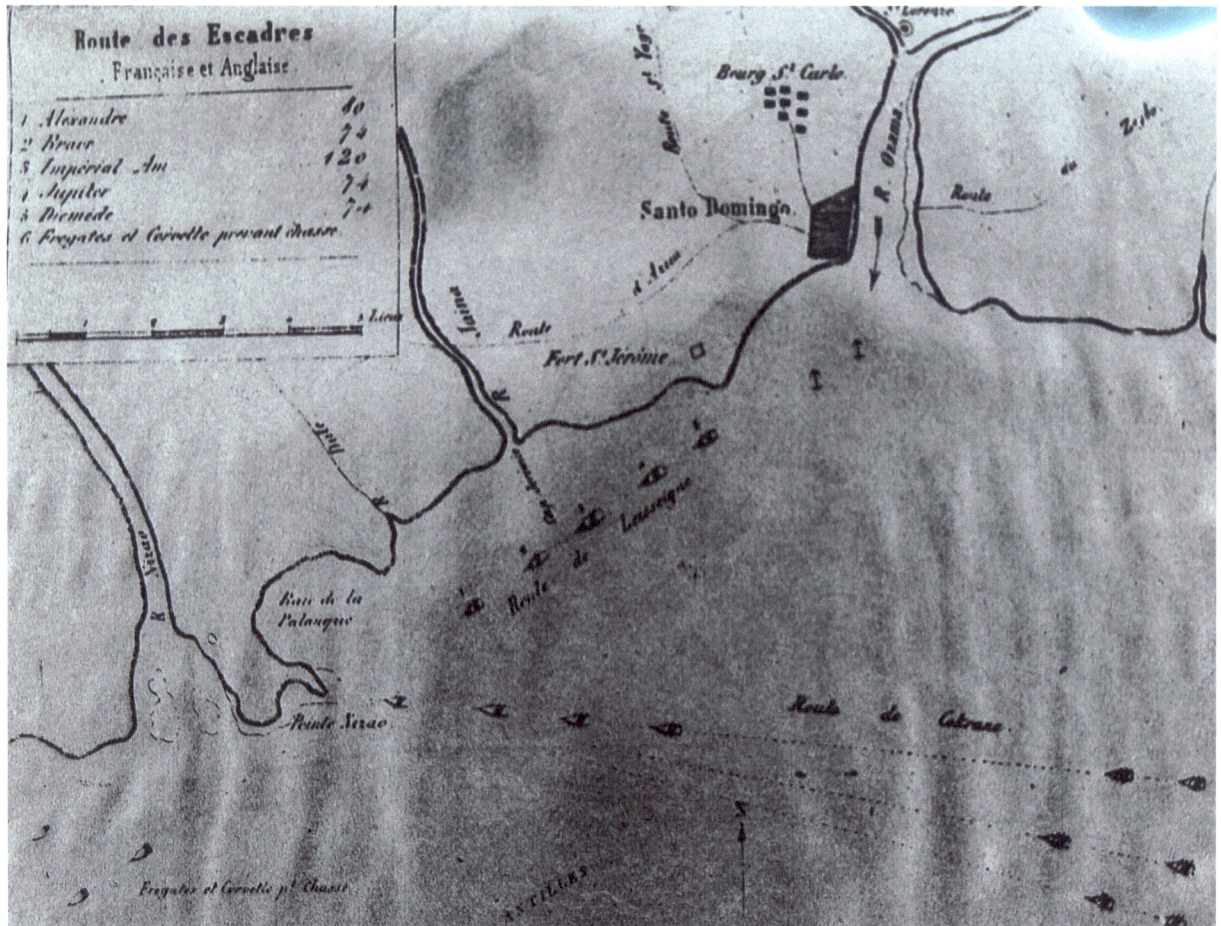

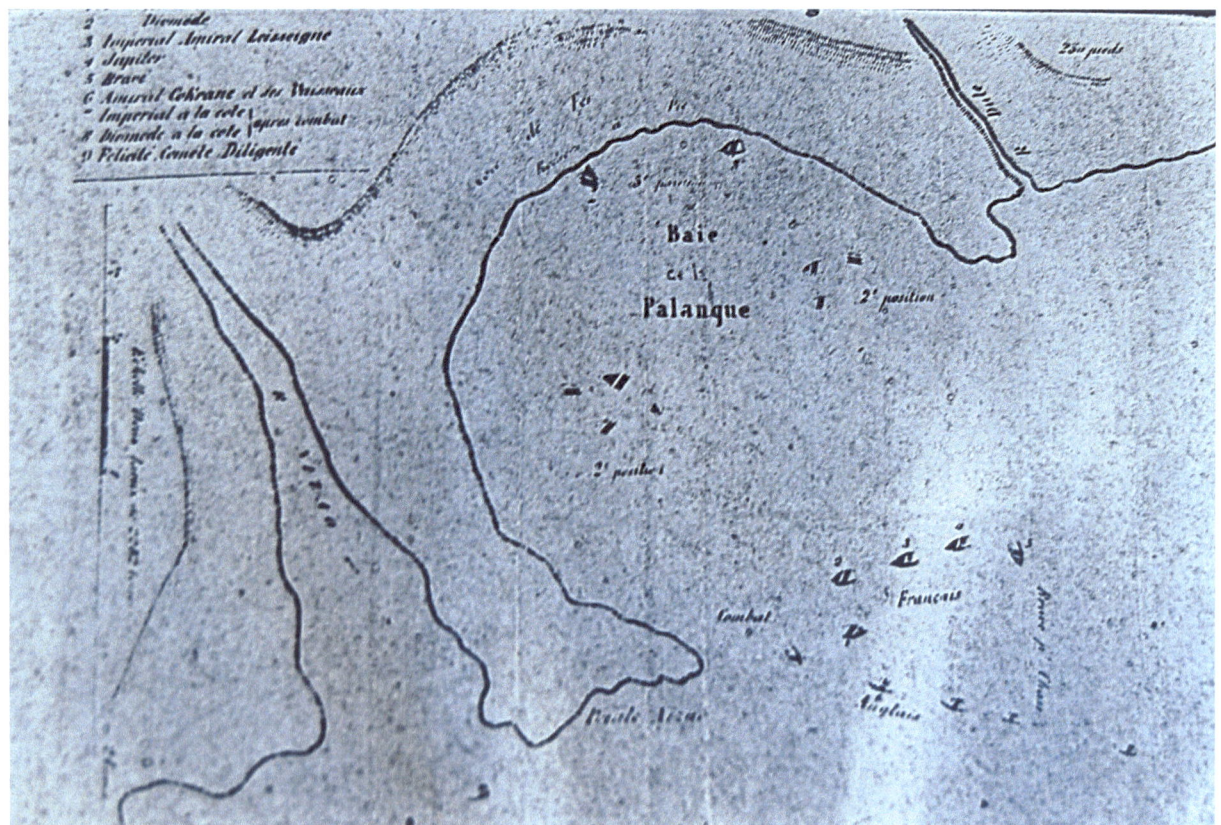

30

This anchor was recovered by a fisherman in the Palenque area several years ago.

The following photo shows one of four swivel cannon recovered in front of the Palenque river several years ago. Note that in 2008, severe rain associated with a hurricane caused a lot of sediment in the river, which has probably covered over the wreck sites. Remote sensing equipment will probably be necessary to locate these shipwrecks.

Note what happens to an iron cannon when not conserved properly

Photo below is another anchor recovered from an unknown wreck in the Palenque area.

Documented shipwrecks in the Palenque – San Pedro area

The shipwrecks listed without coordinates on the following pages are shipwrecks we have found in one or more sources during our research. These shipwrecks are of interest to the authors because with many "unknown" shipwrecks having been discovered in this area, perhaps the information contained herein will help identify one or more of these "unknown" wrecks. Some of the information was obtained from a resource named "Hughes List", which some feel is not totally reliable.

Note that it is estimated that there are over 500 shipwrecks in the waters surrounding the Dominican Republic. This book is not an attempt to document all the shipwrecks; several good books have been written on the subject (Robert F. Marx, *Shipwrecks of the Western Hemisphere*; Dr. Lubos Kordac, *Historic Shipwrecks of the Dominican Republic and Haiti*).

This book is oriented toward documenting shipwrecks that the authors have personally verified exist, including their exact locations. The exceptions are those listed below, which were obtained from research, and which we hope to match up with at least some of the "unknown" wrecks already discovered and those yet to be discovered.

San Bartolome
Comments: 120 ton Nao, in 1556 sank near Santo Domingo, Capt Blas Alonso

> **1556 R**.
> sur la liste, à l'appel final du 15 octobre 1556, 20 restent, 2 manquent, les autres ont disparu au cours du voyage, 2 morts, 1 quitte le navire, aux Canaries.
> (18) Ct. 2898, f° 199 : « el registro original de la nao, Maestre Miguel de La Borda, se ynvió al Consejo de Indias por mandado de S.M. y quedo un treslado del autoriçado en la Contaduría
> (19) Ct. 2898, f° 199 : « viniendo de la ciudad de Santo Domingo arribo a la Ysla Española donde se perdio cerca de la dicha ciudad de Santo Domingo con lo que traya ecebto el oro y plata y algunos cueros que diz que se salvaron ».

The San Juan
Comments: 200 ton Nao, sank en Puerto Hermoso in 1549, Captain Martin de Cavala

> [17] *Ibid.*, I, 1659; III, 694, 695, 696 (mai 1549). Ce navire fait naufrage près de San Domingo « en Puerto Hermoso »; « Jaime de Torregroja, Rodrigo de Baeças, Francisco Ruiz, Pedro Lopez de Toledo, Alonso Fernandez de Melgarejo, Luis Hurtado, Ruy Diaz, etc., todos mercaderes estantes en Sevilla, cargadores que fueron de la nao San Juan.... de la que era maestre y señor Martin de Çavala dan poder a este para que reciba lo que se salvo de la dicha nao ».

The Arrow
Comments: 183 ton Canadian schooner built in 1902 in Liverpool.112 feet x 27 feet. Foundered near Palenque in front of river on 12/22/1907

The HMS Lark
Comments: 18 guns, sank August 3, 1809 - Foundered in a gale off Causada (Point Palenque), the commander, Nicholas, and all but 3 men out of 120 were lost. The ship *Moselle* rescued the survivors

The Elsie

Comments: 149 ton Canadian schooner – 112 feet x 27 feet. Foundered at the mouth of the Palenque river on 06/13/1907

The Blue Jacket

Comments: Canadian schooner built in 1862 in Pictou N.S. Wrecked at Santo Domingo on 09/06/1869

The Clement

Comments: French merchant ship wrecked in 1792 while leaving the port of Santo Domingo – commanding officer Omalin.

The JL Ralston

Comments: 462 ton Canadian schooner – 156 x 35feet. Burned in Santo Domingo harbor on 04/05/1921.

The HMS Flying Fish

Comments: English ship carrying 12 guns, Captain J. Glassford Gooding, wrecked December 15th 1808 east of Point Salinas

---

DID YOU KNOW?

- Spanish "Pieces of Eight" (8 reales) were coins first struck in 1497 containing a high silver purity and weight. They were the basis of the monetary system of the Spanish Empire and were widely circulated around the world. They were accepted as legal tender in the US until 1857

- In Colonial times, lack of small coins often resulted in a "Piece of Eight" (8 reales) being cut into 8 "bits". So, "two bits" was a quarter of a piece of 8 and was subsequently used to refer to a Quarter in US coinage.

- 1770 Iron cross stock was first used on anchors, but not until the mid 1800s was it popular

- from 1492-1830 Spanish mines were in Mexico 40 %, Peru (used to encompass today's Bolivia) 40 %, Colombia and Chile 20 %

- There are over 3,000,000 shipwrecks on the ocean's bottom (source UNESCO)

OTHER AREAS OF THE DOMINICAN REPUBLIC
Juan Dolia

The Tania
Depth: 130 feet maximum depth
Bottom: Sandy hard bottom
Location: 18° 23.266' N 69° 24.944' W
Comments: 200 ft long, sunk in 1999 by Barcelo Capella Resort in Juan Dolio.

San Pedro de Macoris

Unknown Wreck
Depth: Less than 30 feet
Bottom: Sandy, silty bottom
Location: 18°26.142'N 69°18.846'W
Comments: Metal hull and frame

This is another modern wreck grounded near the main road in San Pedro de Macoris

Unknown Wreck

Depth: Less than 35 feet

Bottom: Sandy, silty rocky bottom, some large rocky outcroppings, be careful near channel.

Location: 18° 26. 218' N 69° 18. 826' W

Comments: Hull and boiler still there. This is a dive for advanced divers – near channel.

The Myrtle Leaf

Comments: 336 ton Canadian schooner – 135 feet x 33 feet. Wrecked on 06/12/1919 at San Pedro de Macoris.

The Bianca

Comments: 179 ton Canadian wooden hull schooner built in 1888. Missing on 08/01/1899 after leaving port in San Pedro de Macoris bound for New York with a cargo of sugar.

The Francis

Comments: 159 ton Canadian schooner – 120 feet x 29 feet. Wrecked at San Pedro de Macoris on 08/02/1918

Unknown wreck

Location: 18° 26.135' 69° 17.415' W

Comments: 4 cannon at this site about 200 meters off shore. An anchor is located a little further east of the cannon.

Unknown wreck

Depth: Less than 25 feet

Bottom: Hard bottom with sandy pockets

Location: 18° 26.234' N 69° 18.108' W

Comments: Ballast pile at this location.

Unknown wreck

Depth: Less than 25 feet

Bottom: Reef with sandy areas

Location: 18° 26.000' N 69° 17.744' W

Comments: One cannon 9 feet long at this location.

Bayahabe

The Saint George

Depth: Maximum depth 120 feet

Bottom: Hard bottom with sandy pockets

Location: 18° 20.532' N 68° 49.949' W

Comments: Short boat ride. Hotels in area have dive boats to this dive site.

Boca de Yuma

The Siminal also known as "The Rail Track Wreck"

Depth: Less than 25 feet

Bottom: Hard bottom with sandy pockets

Location: 18° 11.575'N 68° 37.958'W

Comments: May have been a wooden barge - only one anchor and a pile of rail track left

Photos by Thomas Riffaud

El Eleven

Depth: Less than 25 feet
Bottom: Hard bottom with sandy pockets
Location: 18° 12.418'N 68° 38.283'W
Comments: Modern metal ship - great photo opportunity

Photos by Thomas Riffaud

El Beta
Depth: Less than 25 feet
Bottom: Hard bottom with sandy pockets
Location: 18° 17.582'N 68° 37.490'W
Comments: Large scattered steel ship. Local fisherman can take you to this dive site.

Photos by Thomas Riffaud

Unknown wreck
Location: 18° 10.579'N 68° 37.489'W
Comments: Modern wreck on reef near Isla Saona

Unknown wreck
Location: 18° 10.432'N 68° 37.471'W
Comments: Modern wreck on reef near Isla Saona

Photo of the two Unknown wrecks near Isla Saona

Punta Cana

The Astron

Depth: Less than 45 feet, most of wreck is on the reef and out of the water
Location: 18 43 799'N 68 27 256'W

Comments: The *Astron* was a ship that was delivering 60 tons of corn to Cuba, when it ran aground in Punta Cana during a storm. It was a Russian freighter ship that was 120 meters long and broke apart into two pieces with the bow above the water and the stern underwater.

The Monica
Depth: 40 feet maximum depth
Location: 18° 39.265' N 68° 20.806' W

Unknown wreck – possible barge
Location: 18° 53.554'N 68° 39.622'W

The Batey Papagayo
Location: 18° 56.154'N 68° 42.538'W
Comments: Located north of Punta Cana

The "Spoon Wreck"
Location: (restricted)
Comments: The local name "The Spoon Wreck" comes from local fishermen finding many spoons on the site. The anchor shown below is from this site.

Unknown wreck

Location: (restricted)

Comments: Located north of Punta Cana. Two different photos of the same anchor.

OTHER SHIPWRECKS
Labadie Haiti

This is a special area to the author, Black Duck, for reasons that cannot be revealed at this time.

These wrecks are in less than 50 feet of water including the "mung" they are under. It is really easy to get to the site. You can get to them in a ten minute boat ride from the hotels. The best hotel in the area is *The Cormier Plage Resort,* just outside Cap-Haitien.

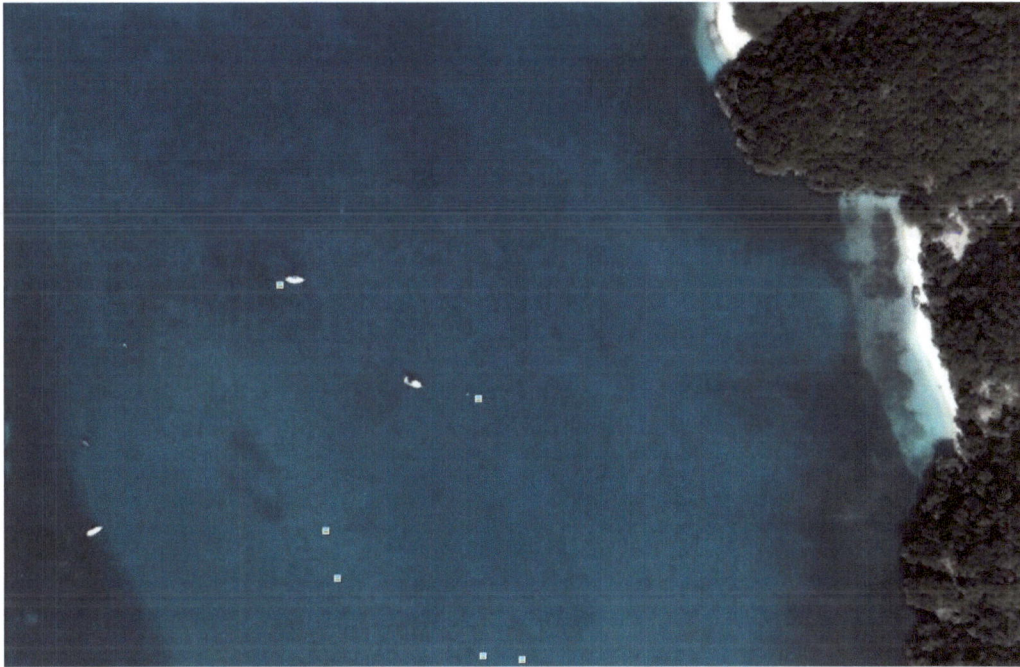

Note the two ballast piles in the lower left

Shot of area near Labadie, Haiti

DID YOU KNOW?

- You can never be 100 % sure what country the ship is from by its cannon. When one ship captured another they would take what was better than they had from the captured ship, including cannon, anchors, etc. Pirate ships were usually ships captured from one country and filled with booty from numerous ships and countries.

- There have been five degrees of **Doctor of Marine Histories** awarded to date, Robert F. Marx, Dr Lee Spence, Peter Throckmorton, and two others were the recipients.

- All the documents predating 1670 that were kept in Old Panama City were destroyed by fire When Henry Morgan and his men burned down the city. All the documents post dating 1670 have been destroyed by the humid climate of the Panama area.

- The Main Archives in Lima, Peru was destroyed twice by earthquakes in the eighteenth century.

- In 1551 a fire destroyed all the records of Spain in the House of Trade building, then again in 1962 by a flood.

- All the records in the archives of Bogota and Cartagena Columbia were destroyed during the war of Independence.

- Since 1740 the best source of information on British shipwrecks is the Lloyd's List.

- Between 1492 and 1830 the Spaniards mined a total of 4,035,156,000 peso of gold and silver in the mines of the New World - 1/10 was gold.

- 98 Percent of all ship wrecks lost in the Western Hemisphere prior to 1825 were lost in shallow water at depths of 30 feet or less.

- In the Mediterranean the opposite is true - 96 percent of all shipwrecks are in 100 feet of water or deeper.

- Ballast rocks can have a metal content and be picked up by a metal detector.

- Fired ceramics, such as olive jars can often be detected with a metal detector.

TREASURE FINDING TECHNIQUES AND EQUIPMENT

In this section we will discuss how to go about being a successful "Treasure Finder", and also discuss the various types of equipment used in the search and salvage of shipwrecks. We don't have experience with all makes and brands, but we have tried out quite a few and our "Equipment Recommendations" section provides some of our experience and our opinions with a variety of equipment. This is not meant to be an exhaustive guide, rather an introduction with references where appropriate.

HOW TO BE SUCCESSFUL AT "TREASURE FINDING"

Key things to being a successful <u>Treasure Finder.</u>

- Have lots of money or you will be a "Treasure Hunter" not a "Treasure Finder". Proper funding and a proper/realistic budget are critical to a successful venture.

- Spending every day that you are on the project being productive. To us this means being a safe, efficient, qualified manager, organizer, coordinator, and running the job.

- Having the right people on the crew. Surround yourself with people that can enhance your project and take it to new levels. A person who knows more than you is not a threat; they are an asset and a blessing. We have had our share of employees over the last 30 years, and one of the worst things you can have is a team member disrupting the project. Everyone has a hidden talent and sometimes it takes a special management and crew to recognize these hidden abilities and put them to good use. However, you have to weigh the good with the bad, and if the person is not a net asset to the company – do the right thing.

- Every morning there should be a status meeting - a discussion about what was accomplished the day before, what will be done this day, any special assignments, any issues or problems that need to be resolved. Everyone needs to know how the team did the day before, and what the expectations are for the day ahead. Any problems need to be addressed and resolved. If you have someone that wants to keep interrupting, telling jokes during the meeting and throughout the day, get rid of them. They are your biggest problem since they will be the one that did not hear anything at the meeting and will put everyone's safety at risk. There are people who are really good at what they do, but if they do not listen, they are a risk and a danger to the rest of the crew; man up and get rid of them.

- Also anyone that says they are an expert at everything and they know how to do everything that is brought up in any conversation, probably doesn't know anything -- get rid of them.

- Strangely enough, one thing we found is that if you do not look, you will not find. We have seen first-hand many treasure or salvage companies that only work a few months out of the year, but live off the investors all year round. To us this is just wrong and unethical. You must get in the water and look before you will find anything.

- Being a good researcher by actually doing your research yourself. It is fine to have someone else doing research for you, but you need to see their sources and documentation. Don't believe something just because someone says it.

- The author would like to note that in his opinion Dr. Lee Spence is the best researcher he knows. Shipwrecks are his passion and part of his lifestyle.

- All businesses must have a budget to succeed. Understand what a budget is and stick to it (this is where 90% of all projects fail). The other 9% of failures come from not understanding the rest of this quote. According to the book, *Are You Ready to Be Your Own Boss?*, 70-90% of all new business ventures close in the first year. We believe the numbers are much higher for treasure hunting ventures, and that there are three primary reasons for this: Lack of proper planning, Lack of a realistic budget, and Lack of experience in both business and treasure hunting.

- There are a lot of different things that make a good and successful TREASURE FINDER. Of course your level of commitment and desire to succeed have a lot to do with the final outcome, but the following things are important to success in this and any undertaking involving the ocean.

  - Understanding safety is probably one of the most important considerations, especially in undersea search and salvage. Proper ongoing training is mandatory and safety should always be number ONE.

  - Having a working knowledge of all size boats from 12 foot to at least 40 and even to 100 foot, depending on the project. People working on a boat without proper knowledge can be a big safety concern and a liability.

  - Of course it is critical that the crew knows how to set up and use the equipment and electronics needed for this type of work such as: magnetometers, sidescan sonar, ROV's, u/w video, underwater cameras, water pumps, air lifts, dredges, tool compressors, scuba tank filling compressors, etc.

etc. Everyone should be familiar with all equipment for redundancy, and you should have at least two crew members who are experts in every piece of equipment that you are using. You never want to have to shut down operations because of one person getting ill or leaving.

- You should have a working knowledge of underwater mapping and survey techniques.

- It is critical that everyone on the crew have an understanding correct Archaeological procedures and techniques, at least to the point that they know not to damage an artifact while trying to salvage/save it. They need to take the time needed to do a correct recovery and have the proper tools to do it. If they don't know how, they should get the appropriate help. A priceless unique artifact can be totally destroyed by an over-eager treasure finder. Having a good knowledgeable Archaeologist on board the boat will save you time and money (the key word here is GOOD).

EQUIPMENT RECOMMENDATIONS (stuff we like)

- GPS - We like the Garmin handheld, and the Humminbird integrated GPS/Chartplottter/Side Imaging sonar is one of the greatest tools for small boats we have found.
- Proton Magnetometer: We like the Marine Magnetics SeaSpy (Overhauser sensor).
- Cesium Magnetometer: We like the Geometrics G-882.
- Metal Detectors: We like both Aquapulse AQ1B and JW Fisher Pulse 8-X, the Aquapulse seems to have better range and is cheaper. We don't like the connectors on the JW Fisher units, nor the fact you have to pay extra to get accessories with connectors.
- Diver Magnetometer: We have only tried the JW Fisher *Diver Mag 1*. It is a Proton Magnetometer that the diver can swim behind. Nice for shallow or rocky/reefy areas where you can't work with a towed mag. The display is hard to see depending on lighting conditions, and using it on land (as shown in their brochure) is quite a chore. It's too heavy to carry very far, and the display is not visible because of location and glare, so you have to depend solely on the audio if using on land.
- Handheld pinpointing magnetometer: We like the Aquascan DX200. It is relatively new on the market, but has proven very useful for pinpointing hits detected with the towed magnetometers and the swim-behind Diver Magnetometer. The DX200 is a Fluxgate magnetometer with directional pinpointing capabilities.
- Hookah systems: We like the Keene compressors, but they are not geared towards saltwater use; they need to have a saltwater option where all the parts are stainless.
- Sidescan sonar: For a small survey boat, we have been quite impressed with the

Humminbird 1197c SI unit. It is really an enhanced Fishfinder, but it is inexpensive compared to towed sidescans and does quite a good job in shallow water. It's rated up to 150 feet but our experience is that it is useful up to about 100 feet. We also like the Edge Tech sidescan sonars for deeper areas and for higher resolution work.

- Tool compressors for airlift etc.: Sullivan 185 cfm.
- Air breathing compressors: Mako 8.5 cfm for the boat (with 4 banks) and 14 cfm (with minimum 6-10 banks) for the shop.
- Water pumps for dredge: 2 to 4 inch with all stainless steel parts and Honda motors.
- Outboard motors: In order of preference--Yamaha hands down , Honda, OMC or Evinrude, Mercury, Suzuki.
- Inboard motors: Yanmar, Caterpillar, John Deer, Detroit.
- Camera equipment: For U/W we like Sony and Amphipico, on land Sony and Nikon.
- Scuba regulators: We like the Scuba Pro Mark version with the G250 2nd stage.
- B/C: we like back mounted and side mount.
- Scuba tanks: 120 steel, 80 and 40 aluminum.
- Icom marine radios.
- Submerge Under water Scooters.
- Dive Rite dry suits.
- Light Monkey dive lights - hands down, and the Princeton Tec tech 40 but they are fading out fast.
- Mares fins.
- Richie Wet Notes for Surveying.
- Suunto Compass for site work and surveys.
- Lufkin 100 to 300 feet or 30 to 100 meters vinyl tapes for underwater surveying.
- Snap on wrenches or something equal.
- Coleman coolers.

DID YOU KNOW?

- Although early inventors, including Leonardo da Vinci and Giovanni Alfonso Borelli, toyed with the concept of swimfins, Benjamin Franklin invented the modern swimfin in 1717 at age 12

EQUIPMENT INFORMATION AND DISCUSSION

FIRST AID KIT

Safety First! Both on the boats and in the lab, have good First Aid Kits! And what goes hand-in-hand with having a good First Aid Kit is having people that know how to use them. Everyone on your crew should be trained in First Aid and also be CPR certified.

GPS

If you want to find wrecks then read this! Not everyone knows how this works. We have found experienced boat captains that don't have a clue about much of what we shall explain in this section.

A common scenario: You are given a set of GPS coordinates from a friend for a hot fishing spot or a possible wreck site. You take the coordinates, plug them into your GPS and head out to the spot, but when you get there – you can't find it. You know you are right on the spot, your GPS says so, but there is nothing there except flat sandy bottom. What went wrong?

It is not uncommon for two or three people to put the same coordinates into their respective GPS's and hit "GO TO" as they head to their destination. As they draw near, they find that they are all going to different places, some as much as two miles apart. What causes that? Well the answer is pretty simple, but you would be surprised at how many people using a GPS today don't know what is explained below.

Here are the two very basic things that MUST be checked if you are to be successful with a GPS:

1. POSITION
2. MAP DATUM

POSITION. In your GPS there is something called "Position", usually found in the setup menu. You will find the following three options among others:

- Lat/Lon hddd°mm.mmm (h=hemisphere, ddd=degrees of latitude or longitude, mm.mmm=minutes of latitude or longitude expressed to 1/1,000[th] of a minute)

- Lat/Lon hddd°mm'ss.s" (h=hemisphere, ddd=degrees of latitude or longitude, mm=minutes of latitude or longitude, ss.s=seconds of latitude or longitude expressed to 1/10th of a second)

- Lat/Lon hddd.ddddd° (h=hemisphere, ddd.ddddd=degrees of latitude or longitude expressed to 1/10,000[th] of a degree)

It is critical that you know the Position format of the coordinates someone gives you. If they give you one format and your GPS is set to another format, it will be confusing to try to enter the coordinates, and if you do enter them in some fashion, they will be WRONG. ALWAYS make sure you are talking "apples to apples".

Map Datum. Map Datum refers to various versions of geodetic datum that have been established over the years. A geodetic datum is the tool used to define the shape and size of the earth, as well as the reference point for the various coordinate systems used in mapping the earth. Throughout time, hundreds of different datums have been used - each one changing with the earth views of the times.

Modern GPS technology supports many Map Datums and allows switching back and forth between them. The critical thing for the GPS user to know is WHAT MAP DATUM WAS USED FOR THE COORDINATES he has been given. If someone recorded coordinates on a GPS set to one Map Datum and you enter those coordinates in your GPS, which is set to a different Map Datum, you could be off by as much as a mile or more.

Datums commonly in use today are: WGS 84, WGS 72, NAD27, NAD83, just to name a few. Most GPS units and chart/map software have well over 100 Map Datum selections. The most common settings in use today are: **WGS 84 Datum and Position set to hddd° mm.mmm**

To be successful with a GPS:

1. Always have your GPS set to whatever the Position and Map Datum were set at when the sites where recorded.

2. If you are getting GPS coordinates off paper charts/maps, LOOK ON THE CHART OR MAP FOR THE MAP DATUM, and make sure your GPS is set to the same Map datum.

3. When using Google Earth or Garmin Mapsource, or other mapping software, make sure the software settings for Position and Map Datum match those of your GPS. Here's what you will see in the Google Earth setup:

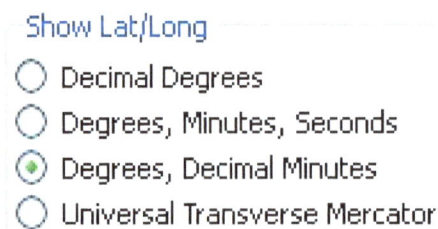

Show Lat/Long
○ Decimal Degrees
○ Degrees, Minutes, Seconds
⦿ Degrees, Decimal Minutes
○ Universal Transverse Mercator

4. When all else fails, READ THE MANUAL? Black Duck says the manuals don't tell you what you need to know, and he's right. I looked in the Garmin manual and it says, *"To access the Units Setup page: From the Setup Menu, select Units. Position Format—sets the coordinate system in which a location is shown. Map Datum—sets the description for geographic location for, mapping, and navigation and is not an actual map in the unit."* Well, I must agree with Black Duck, that just doesn't tell you all you need to know; thus the need for our book.

Similar setups will be found on mapping software, survey software, and other software similar to Google Earth. If you use this type of software, be sure your configuration setups in the software match your GPS settings to avoid confusion and errors.

Depth Sounder

Depth Sounders, echo sounders, or fathometers should be the second piece of equipment acquired before conducting a search in the ocean. It is necessary, not only to indicate the depth, but also to prevent the survey or salvage vessel from becoming a shipwreck statistic itself in shallow, reef or rock-strewn waters. It helps locate shoals, rocks, and reefs where ships may have wrecked. Many of the modern depth sounders are used by fishermen to locate reefs and rocks where fish may be more plentiful. Some of them produce an image of the bottom showing a great deal of detail. In the past decade, two of the richest Chinese porcelain wrecks, both lying between 120 and 140 feet deep, were located using only a depth sounder.

Magnetometers

Magnetometers, which detect the presence of ferrous metal, have been the main search tool used for locating old shipwrecks, especially those that are buried under sediment or coral, and for shipwrecks where visual search is restricted for whatever reason. Magnetometers are also used for confirming targets, which have been located with sidescan sonar, when the operator is not certain if the target is a shipwreck or a natural anomaly. Any magnetometer, however, is only as good as the skill of the operator running it. Many shipwrecks have been missed by incompetent magnetometer users.

Basically, a magnetometer detects gradients or localized distortions in the earth's magnetic field produced by local concentrations of ferro-magnetic materials such as cannon, anchors or any other ferrous metal objects on a shipwreck. The larger the object is and the longer it has remained in the same position, the better the chances are of locating it with a magnetometer.

There are numerous types of magnetometers available today, each working on a different principle: Proton Precession, Rubidium, Overhauser, Alkali Vapor, Rotating Coil, Hall Effect, Fluxgate, Caesium Vapor, to name a few. The most common types used for locating shipwrecks are Proton Precession, Overhauser, Caesium, and Fluxgate. The authors have personally used both the Proton Precession and the Overhauser magnetometers to search for shipwrecks. Magnetometer measurements are made in nanoteslas (nt) which are often called "gamma". The standard Proton magnetometer achieves a 1nt resolution, whereas the Overhauser magnetometer achieves a 0.01nt resolution. The Overhauser magnetometer also has the added benefits of using much less power and it is not affected by location or direction, nor is it as susceptible to noise as the Proton magnetometer.

Marine magnetometer surveys are generally performed by towing the magnetometer sensor (towfish) behind a boat at a speed between 3 and 10 knots. Before the advent of the GPS, survey areas were marked off with buoys and the survey boat attempted to run parallel grid lines based on the buoys and compass readings. Older magnetometers either had no recording capability, or they printed readings on a paper roll. Today, sophisticated computer software is available that interfaces with the magnetometer and a GPS, giving the boat pilot a visual grid to follow, with the boat's position shown at all times. The magnetometer data is constantly recorded on a laptop or desktop computer along with the GPS data, and may be played back for review at a later time.

Top photo at right is a SeaSpy Magnetometer towfish from Marine Magnetics. The SeaSpy uses the Overhauser technology.

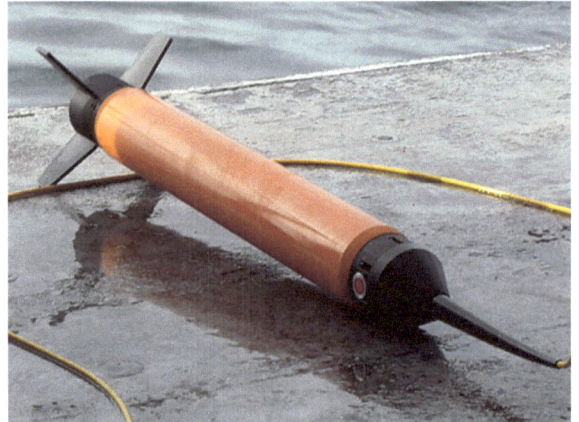

The bottom photo is a Geometrics G-882 cesium-vapor marine magnetometer towfish.

The configurations for using magnetometers in shallow water (less than 100 feet deep) and deep water vary considerably. In shallow water, the length of cable required is usually 100 meters or less. This can be readily handled manually and the magnetometer towfish can be deployed and retrieved manually. At greater depths, the cable must be much longer and thus much heavier. The increased weight requires mechanical equipment to pay out and retrieve the cable and towfish. The

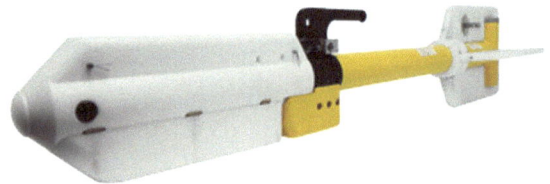

towfish must also be able to withstand the pressure of the greater depths. Shallow water surveys can generally be accomplished from small skiffs, whereas deep water surveys are generally performed by larger boats with electric winches to pay out and retrieve the towfish.

The grids or lanes used to perform a magnetometer survey are spaced, depending on the target. A 300 ton steel ship can be detected from over 1,000 feet away. So, if you are searching for a target of that size, your lanes could be every 500 feet or even more. An older wooden shipwreck with a large number of iron cannon and anchors may be detected from 200 to 300 feet away, if the iron objects are confined to one small area. When the wreck has been scattered and large ferrous articles broadcast over a large area, each piece will probably be detected at a maximum range of 100 feet. In cases where a shipwreck has only small ferrous items such as cannonballs, tools, weapons, and bits of rigging, the location will be detected only if the sensing probe passes within 30 or 40 feet of the site. If very small items are widely scattered, the probe must come within 10 to 15 feet to detect them.

As you can see, knowledge of your target is very important (Did it have bronze or iron cannon? Did it sink in a storm, and thus would more likely be scattered? Is the area where it sank subject to frequent storms or hurricanes, and if so, it would more likely be scattered?). The time it takes to do a magnetometer survey depends on the speed and the width of the lanes. If you want to make certain you don't miss targets that can only be detected if you are within 10 or 15 feet, then your lanes must be no more than about 15 feet and your sensor has to be towed within about 10 feet of the bottom. This can be very challenging in an area that is rocky, has large coral growths, or has variable depths. In a fixed depth, flat, sandy bottom environment, a survey is very simple. Otherwise it takes an experienced operator to perform a survey and gather meaningful data while, avoiding damaging the towfish or cable on rocks or reefs.

The image below shows the magnetometer "hit" that discovered the ballast pile of the Nuestra Señora de la Consolación shipwreck at Santa Clara Island in Ecuador. Produced with an Aquascan AX2000 Proton Magnetometer – used with permission - William G. Seliger.

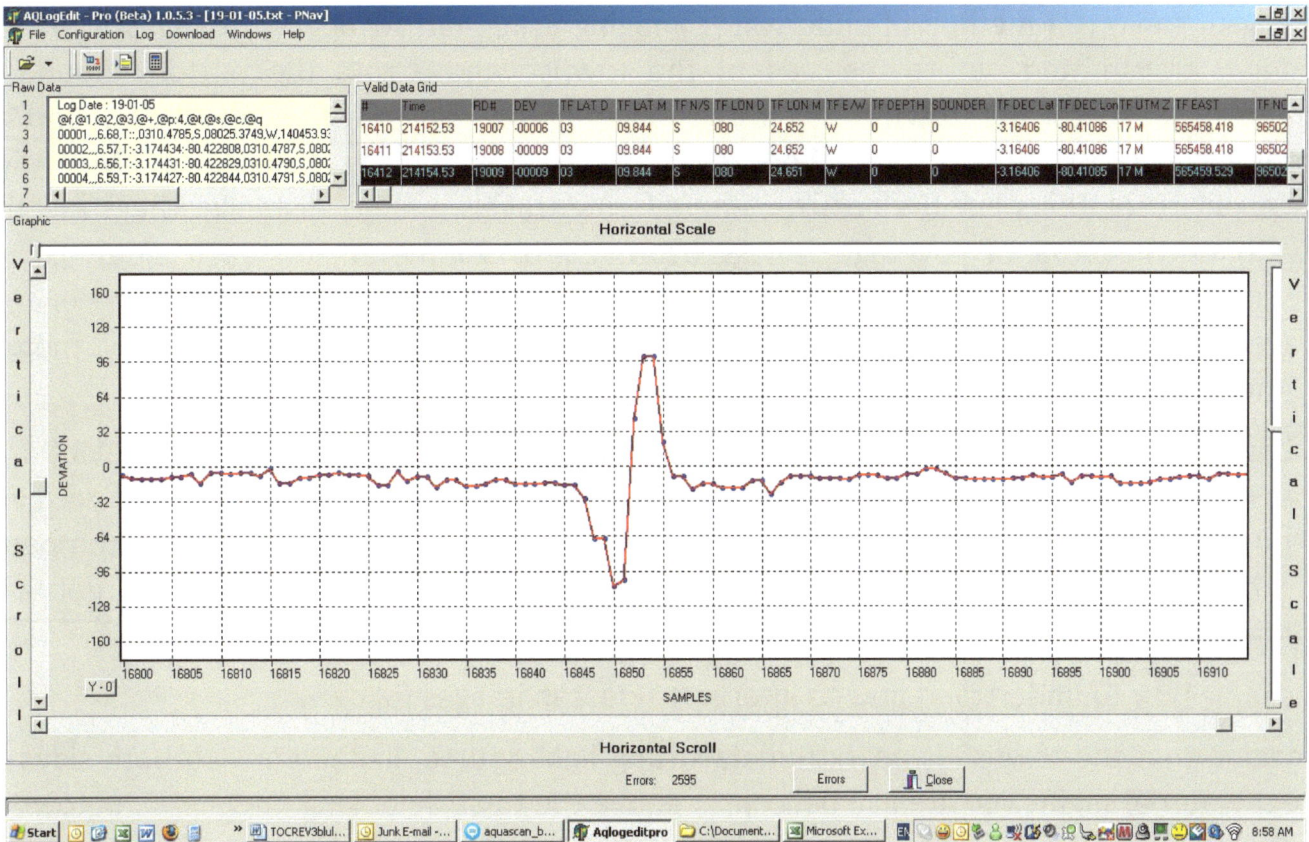

Handheld or Swim-behind Magnetometers

Several manufacturers produce a small hand held magnetometer that can be utilized by a diver to search for ferrous objects, or to pinpoint an object detected with the towed magnetometer. These have proven very useful when the shipwreck is totally covered in sand since the diver can pinpoint exactly the spot with the handheld device and then bring in the appropriate equipment to excavate.

We are familiar with the JW Fisher *Diver Mag 1*, a "swim-behind" Proton Magnetometer (shown above) that can be used as both a primary survey tool in circumstances where a towed magnetometer is not feasible; and as a pinpointing tool as well. There are several Fluxgate magnetometers on the market which are made in a gradiometer configuration to give directional pinpointing capabilities. The Aquascan DX-200 is one such device. These are primarily used for pinpointing targets detected with towed magnetometers. We have heard of a diver Cesium magnetometer also, but have no knowledge of it.

Sidescan Sonars

Sidescan sonar is a method of underwater imaging using narrow beams of acoustic energy (sound) transmitted out to the side of the towfish and across the bottom. Sound is reflected back to the towfish from the bottom and objects present there. Certain frequencies work better than others, high frequencies such as 500kHz to 1MHz give excellent resolutions but the acoustic energy only travels a short distance, therefore the swath or the area of coverage is less (from 25 to 75 meters on each side). Lower frequencies such as 50kHz or 100kHz give lower resolution but the distance that the energy travels is greatly improved and therefore the area of coverage is much greater (250 meters or more on each side).

A basic Side Scan Sonar System consists of a topside processing unit, a cable for electronic transmission and towing, and a subsurface unit (a towfish) that transmits and receives acoustic energy for imaging. As stated earlier, most modern units interface to a computer and provide sophisticated software tools for providing the exact GPS position of targets and for calculating the target's dimensions.

A simple way to understand how to interpret sidescan images follows:

Imagine that the towfish is an extremely strong light source, illuminating to both sides in clear water at night. You are in a helicopter above the towfish looking down. As the towfish moves along and illuminates objects on the bottom of the ocean, you can see the objects, which reflect the light and you will see dark shadows behind each object (from the perspective of the light source).

The following diagrams illustrate this concept.

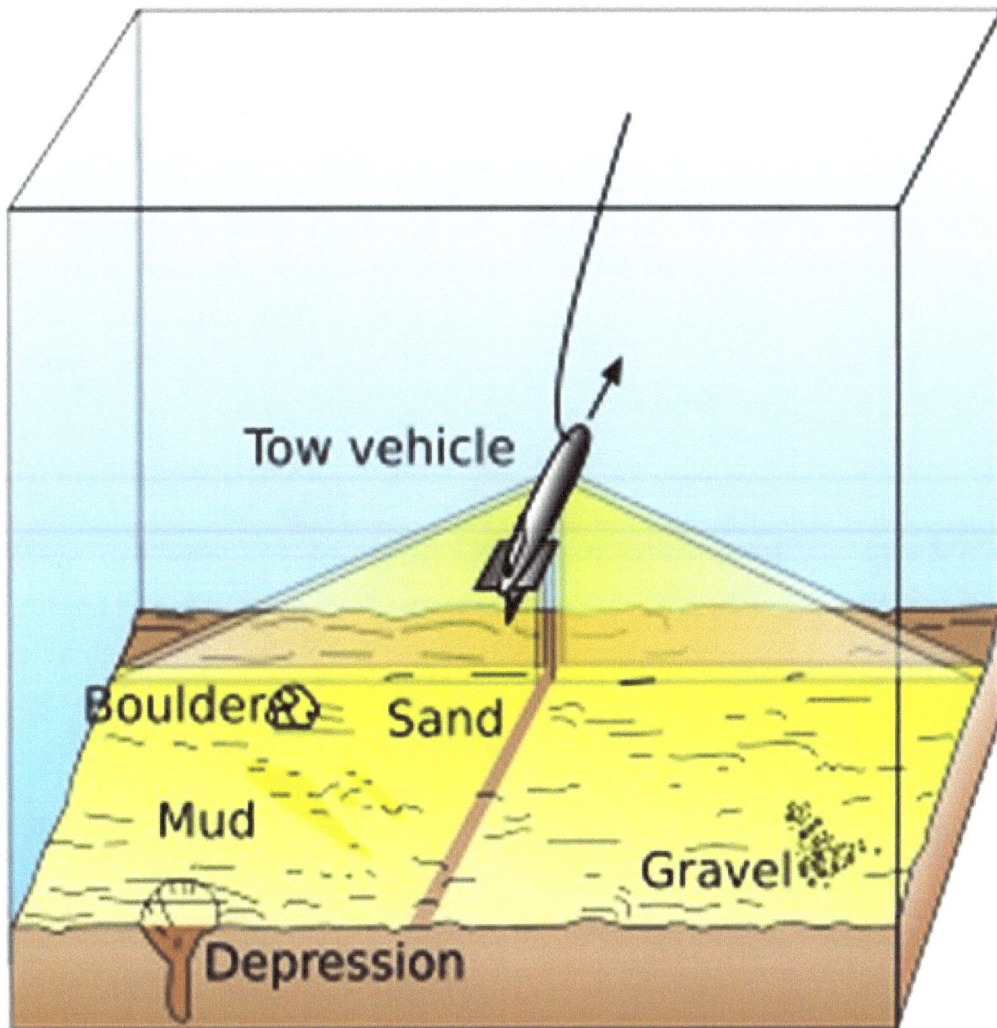

Diagram representing the swath coverage of a sidescan sonar

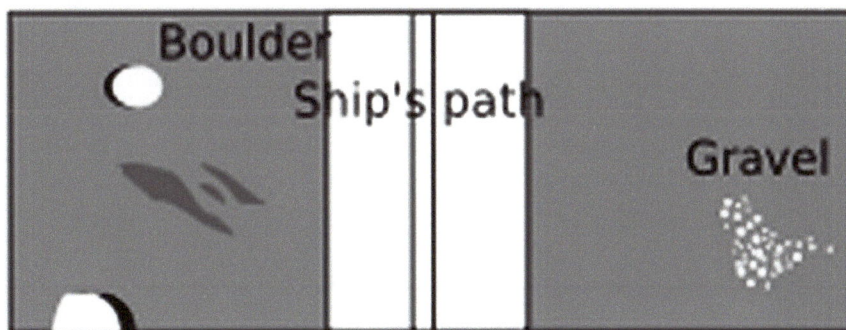

Diagram representing the resulting image from the objects shown in the swath coverage diagram above

In a basic sidescan sonar, the towfish generates one pulse of energy at a time and waits for the sound to be reflected back. The imaging range is determined by how long the towfish waits before transmitting the next pulse of acoustic energy. The image is thus built up one line of data at a time. In a standard monochrome image, hard objects reflect more energy causing a light representation on the image; soft objects that do not reflect energy as well show up as shades of grey. The absence of sound, such as the areas behind an object (referred to as shadows), show up as black areas on a sonar image (see example above). Modern sidescan sonars offer a wide range of color options and filters which can be utilized to enhance the images produced. Recent advances in sidescan technology have options for multiple simultaneous pulses on multiple frequencies, therefore allowing for greater survey speed and both high and low resolution images at the same time.

Sidescan sonar is mainly used for locating ships lost in waters deeper than 100 feet, since the bulk of such a ship will be on the sea floor, not buried under bottom sediment or scattered by storms and wave action. Exceptions occur, however, that make this type of sonar useful for shallow water shipwrecks.

The following images were produced using a color scheme presenting a more natural appearance by having the shadows appear black, and the harder objects reflecting in lighter tones. An experienced sidescan technician is required to interpret the many images produced by sidescan sonar. However, some are readily identifiable. These images show wrecks in varying degrees of deterioration. Images produced by Edge Tech Sidescan sonars, provided courtesy of Edge Tech.

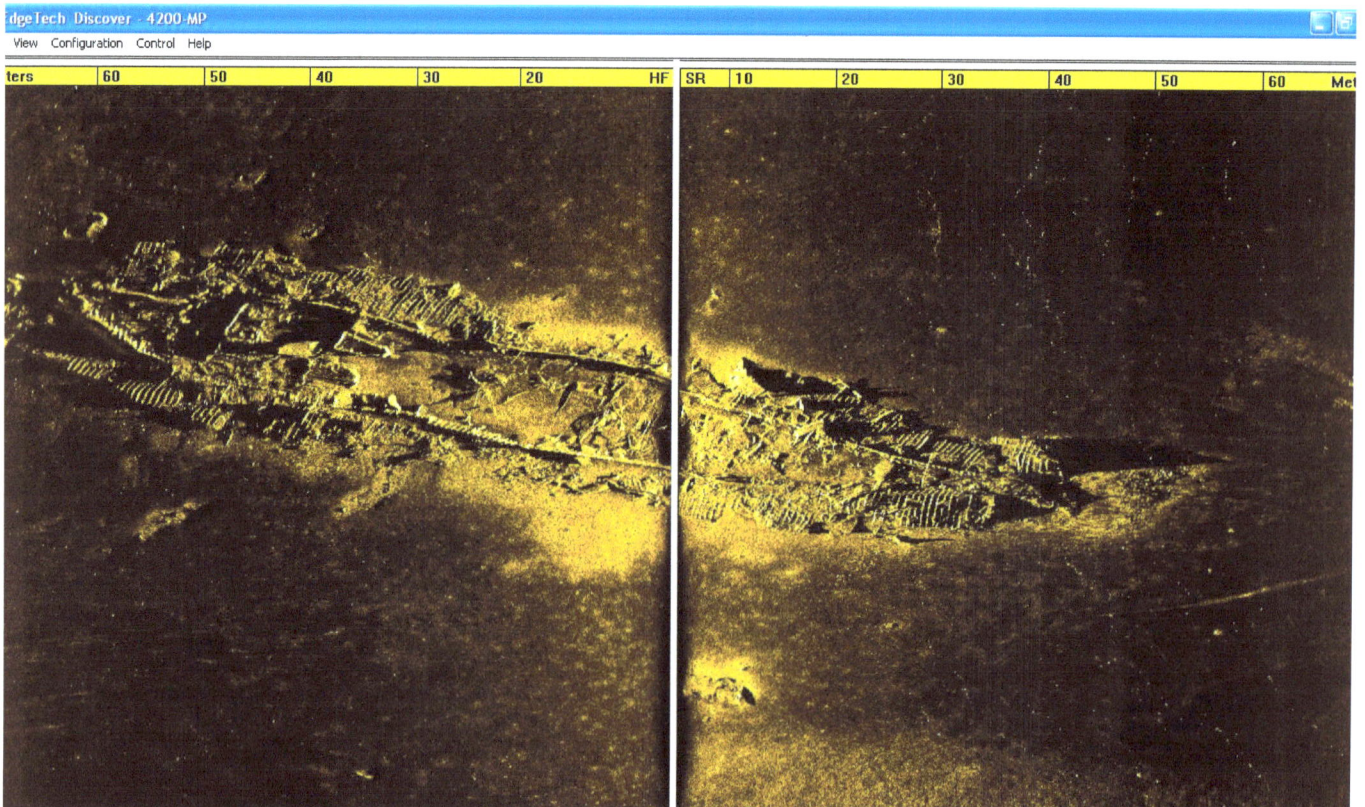

Image of an old deteriorated shipwreck courtesy of Edge Tech

30 | 25 | 20 | 15 | 10

Sidescan image courtesy of Edge Tech

Sub Bottom Profiler

Sub Bottom Profilers, also known as sub-bottom penetrating sonar, are systems used to identify and characterize layers of sediment or rock under the seafloor. The technique used is similar to a simple echo sounder. A transducer emits a sound pulse vertically downwards towards the seafloor, and a receiver records the return of the pulse, once it has been reflected off the seafloor. Parts of the sound pulse will penetrate the seafloor and be reflected off of the different sub-bottom layers and any objects present. The processing unit then converts these energy flections into a visual image.

Sub-bottom sonar is very useful once a shipwreck has been located. This instrument allows archaeologists to develop an effective plan for excavation and management of an underwater archaeological location.

Software

Survey Software

Survey Software is software that provides tools for performing an organized and logical approach to your search. With the advent of the GPS and its interface into the computer, a whole new level of sophistication in treasure hunting has been created. It is now possible to lay out a search grid with lanes drawn according to your specific needs.

The remote sensing equipment available today all come with software which interfaces with GPS technology and which records the survey data onto a computer for later replay and analysis. This type of software technology provides a visual, user-friendly interface to the equipment which gives the user a level of accuracy never achievable before. It is common to identify a possible target on a sidescan sonar image, obtain the GPS coordinates provided by the software, and have a diver go to those coordinates and be within a few feet or meters of the object in question.

Below is an actual screen shot of a search grid set up at an angle to work between two points of land, utilizing a software package called Pnav. This software, produced by Effective Solutions Data Products, has many features to aid with sidescan sonar and magnetometer surveys, including data recording, towfish offset calculations, swath display, etc.

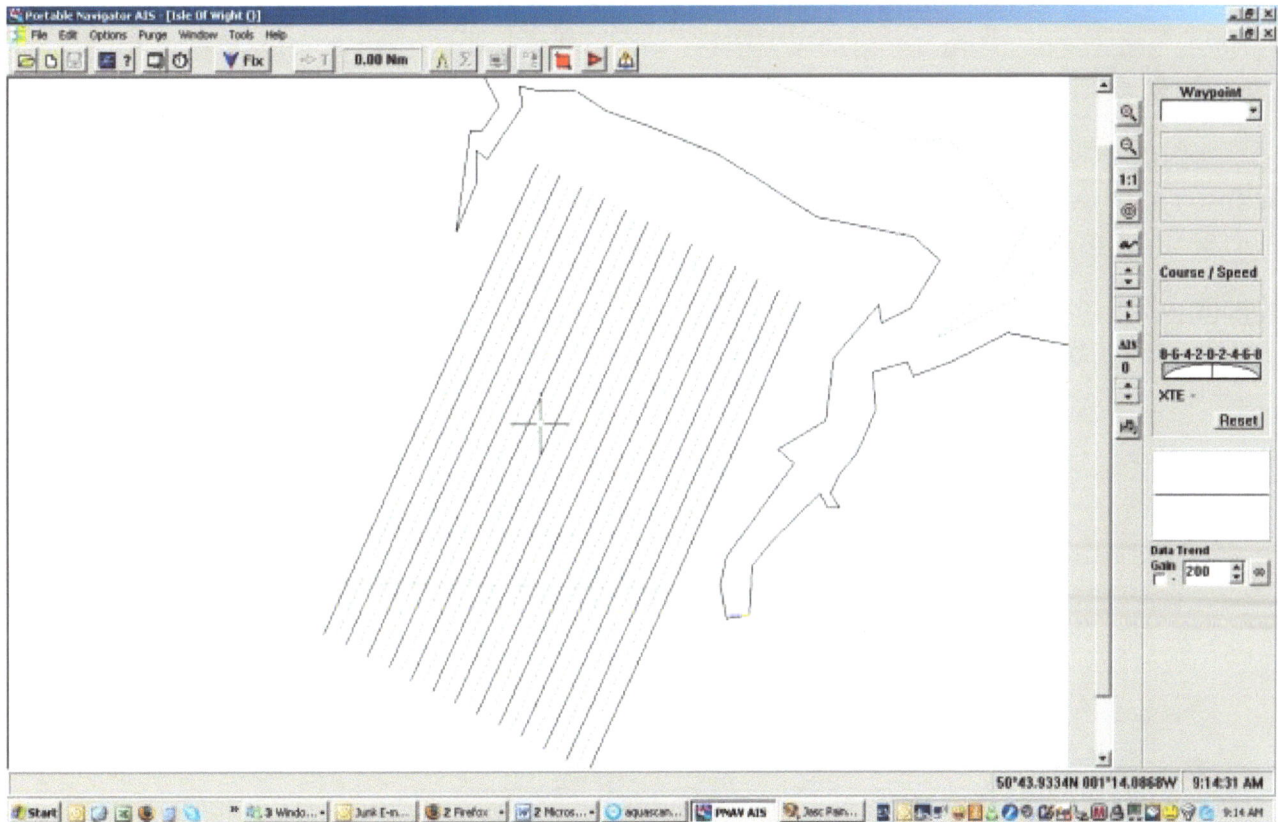

Chart with search grid laid out. When doing a survey, the boat's position is shown and a track of the area covered is also displayed. Pnav software from Effective Solutions Data Products.

GIS Software

GIS Software or "Geographic Information System" software is mapping software that links information as to where things are, with information about what the things are like.

As on the paper map, a digital map created by GIS will have dots, or points, that represent features on the map such as cities; lines that represent features such as roads; and small areas that represent features such as lakes. The difference is that this information comes from a database and is shown only if the user chooses to show it.

Each piece of information in the map sits on a layer, and the users turn on or off the layers according to their needs. One layer could be made up of all the roads in an area. Another could represent all the lakes in the same area. Yet another could represent all the cities.

When excavating a shipwreck using archaeological excavation methods, each item recovered is part of a layer within the shipwreck site. As artifacts are recovered, and their associated data is entered into the GIS, a series of layers are constructed that allow each item recovered to be associated with every other item.

GIS also provides a capability known as spatial analysis. This capability will allow relative distances between artifacts to be stored and interpolated as a means of interpreting archaeological information.

A GIS, properly implemented, coupled with sound excavation and documentation procedures, provides archaeologists with an especially powerful tool for effective study and management of archaeological excavations.

The following images are samples of what can be done with GIS software. These images were provided by 3H Consulting Ltd., and were produced by their software package Site Recorder.

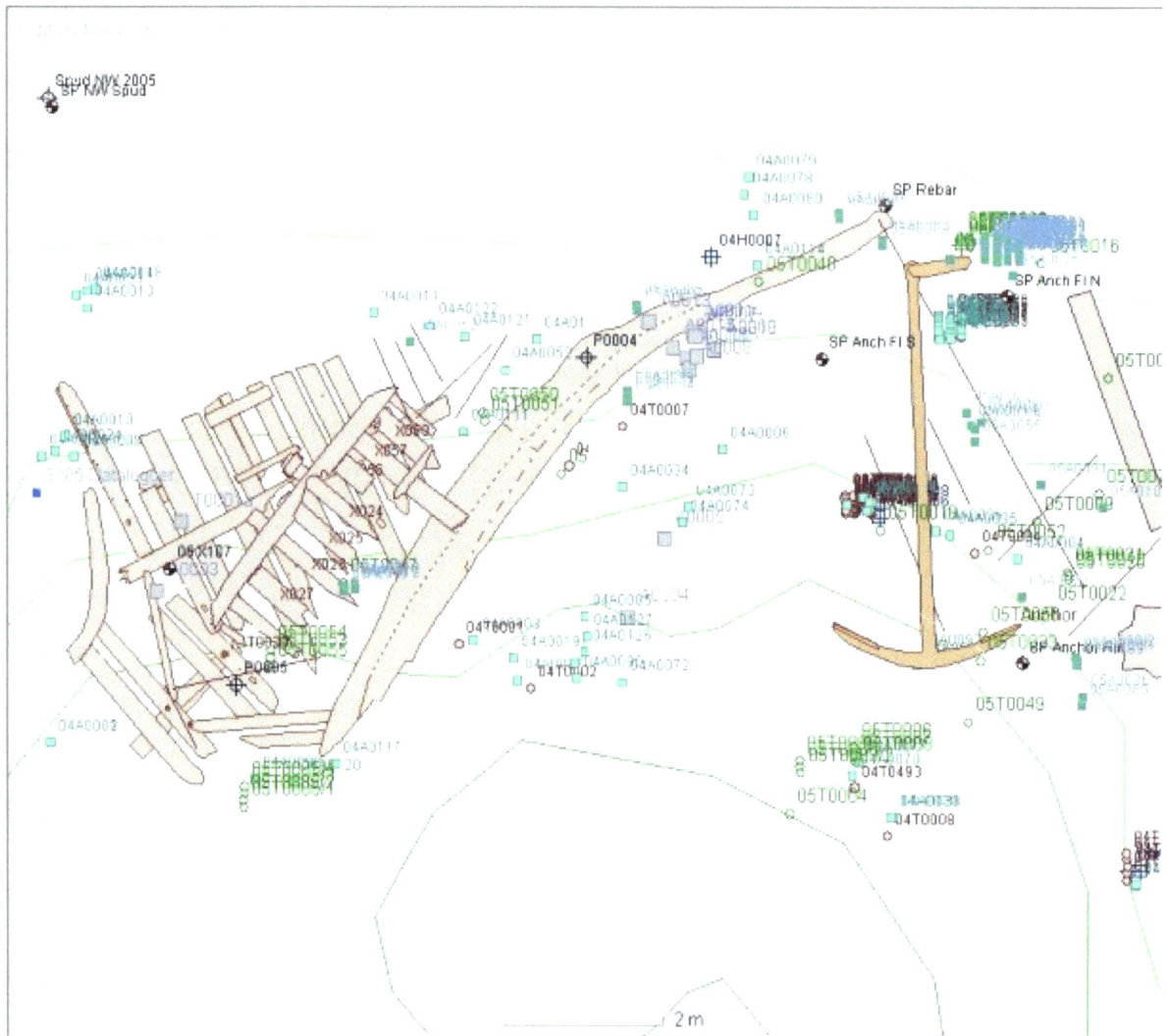

Site Recorder example from shipwreck Mary Rose

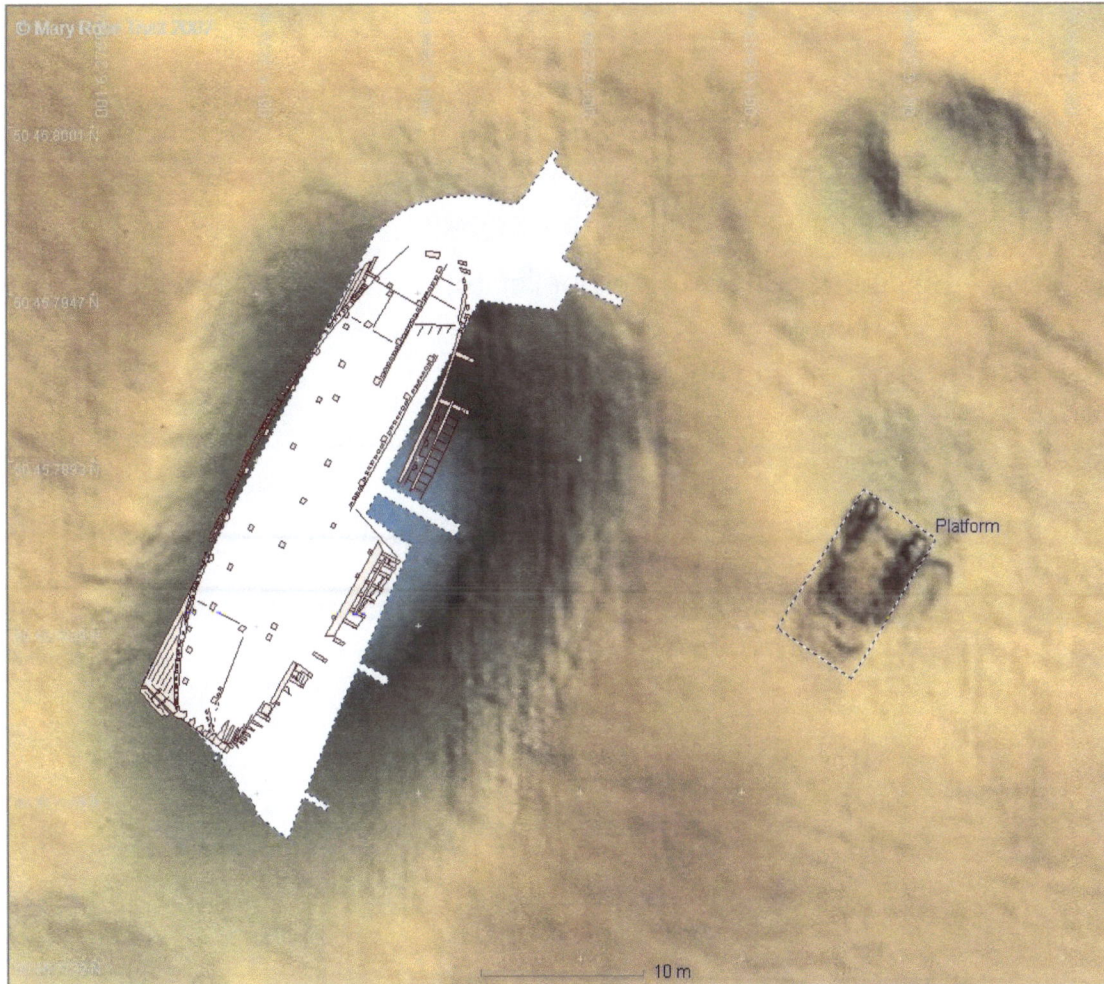

Site Recorder example from the shipwreck Mary Rose

DID YOU KNOW?
• 3000 BC - the first major silver mines were founded in Anatolia, modern day Turkey.
• 1st Century AD Roman discoveries allowed Spain to become a major silver producer.
• Early 1500s - After Columbus' New World expeditions, the discovery of huge, prolific silver deposits in Mexico, Peru and Bolivia changed the focus of silver mining and enriched the Spanish Empire for 300 years.
•

The Blower or "Mailbox"

Blowers (also known as "Mailboxes") are one of the main tools utilized in areas less than 50 feet deep of water where there is a significant amount of overburden to be removed. Mel Fisher is generally credited with inventing this technique.

Originally it was intended to deflect the propeller thrust towards the bottom to carry clear water to the divers working in poor visibility. It worked so well that it began to excavate holes in the bottom sediment and uncover treasure.

Over the years the design has been improved, and it is one of the primary ways you can recognize a "treasure hunting ship" today. If it has one or more giant tubes with 90 degree bends in them mounted on the stern, then it is most likely a treasure hunting/salvage vessel.

Two treasure vessels – The *Dare* (3 blowers) and The *JB Magruder* (2 large blowers)

Close-up of the blowers on the *Dare* (left) and *Magruder* (right)

Blower design and construction is not a simple task. Many things need to be considered and engineered correctly. A few items to consider: the extreme pressure exerted on the blower by the prop wash and where and how the blower is connected to the boat (if not done correctly you will destroy the blower or worse, the boat), clearance for the rudder(s), safety cage to prevent accidents (divers, hookah hoses), how to raise and lower quickly (if bad weather comes upon you rapidly, you don't want a 1 hour job to raise the blowers – you can't get the boat underway with the blowers down), how far behind the prop plane do you want the blower, and a secure and safe (for the divers) mechanism to secure them in the down position.

The Air Lift

The Air Lift is often employed to work a shipwreck site, especially where mud, sand, gravel and small stones need to be cleared away, or where visibility or other conditions dictate that the sediment be lifted to the surface for screening. This is especially useful when the items being sought cannot be detected with any sort of detector. A good example is the "Emerald City" cite of the Atocha. Air lifts are used to bring the bottom sediment to the surface vessel, where it passes through various screens, and then is visually inspected by people with a trained eye for spotting emeralds.

Air lifts come in two types; both work on the same principle. The simplest type acts like a vacuum cleaner, sucking up the bottom sediment, sand, shells, small rocks, and sometimes small treasure artifacts. It has a discharge tube, which can be as short as ten feet or may be much longer, with or without a flexible section at the discharge end. The debris is spewed back into the ocean at the discharge end of the tube and the current carries away the fine particles and sand. Generally, two or three divers work this type of airlift, one manning the airlift tube, one watching for artifacts where the airlift is being utilized and removing those items too large to enter the airlift, and one diver at the discharge end of the tube watching for coins or other artifacts that got sucked up by the airlift. Implementation of this type of airlift requires some visibility to be useful and productive.

In the absence of visibility or in other conditions that warrant lifting the "vacuumed" sediment to the surface for examination, a more complicated airlift may be utilized. This implementation requires more sophisticated positioning and anchoring of the surface vessel since the discharge tube will carry the sediment to the top and actually out of the water and onto the vessel (usually into a mesh basket or screening mechanism). The discharge tube is generally constructed out of a combination of rigid and flexible sections of tubing. This type of airlift has limitations on the amount of movement of the surface vessel that can be tolerated without disrupting the airlift operation. Usually, some type of small anchor blocks are required to keep the discharge tube from being swept away by the current. So, the airlift with topside discharge is more complicated and more expensive to implement and use, but both type work on the same principle as explained below.

Air lifts generally work well where there is 30 feet or more of water. They can be utilized in as little as 15 feet, but their suction ability is greatly diminished in the shallower depths. Air lifts work on the principle that compressed air released under water will rise towards the surface, and while rising towards the surface, the water pressure decreases and the volume of air increases as it expands. An air compressor on the surface vessel pumps compressed air down to the airlift "vacuum tube" (which may be any tube with a diameter of 2 inches to 12 or more inches depending on the situation. A standard airlift tube is generally 4 to 6 inches in diameter). The compressed air is fed into the airlift tube near the bottom and immediately begins to rise towards the surface, expanding and filling the tube as it does. This creates a vacuum effect at the bottom of the airlift tube, and sand, rocks, and other small items in the sediment are lifted along with the air and water in the tube. The deeper the airlift is implemented, the stronger the suction because the air is rising more distance and expanding more as it does. Divers at 60 to 90 feet of depth have reported airlifts sucking up 12 to 16 pound cannonballs with no problem. As explained above, this suction force is enough to lift the bottom sediment up out of the water and deposit it on a boat.

The following table shows the Supply Hose diameter, Air Pressure, and Cubic Feet per Minute air flow required for a 3", 4", and 6" air lift at different working depths.

Airlift Tube Diameter	Supply Hose Diameter	Max Working Depth (feet)	Air Volume (CFM)	PSI Air Pressure
3-inch	½ inch	40	20-40	50
		65	30-50	75
		90	50-60	100
4-inch	¾ inch	40	30-50	50
		65	40-60	75
		90	50-70	100
6-inch	1 inch	40	75-100	50
		65	100-125	75
		90	125-150	100

The diagrams below illustrate the two types of airlifts.

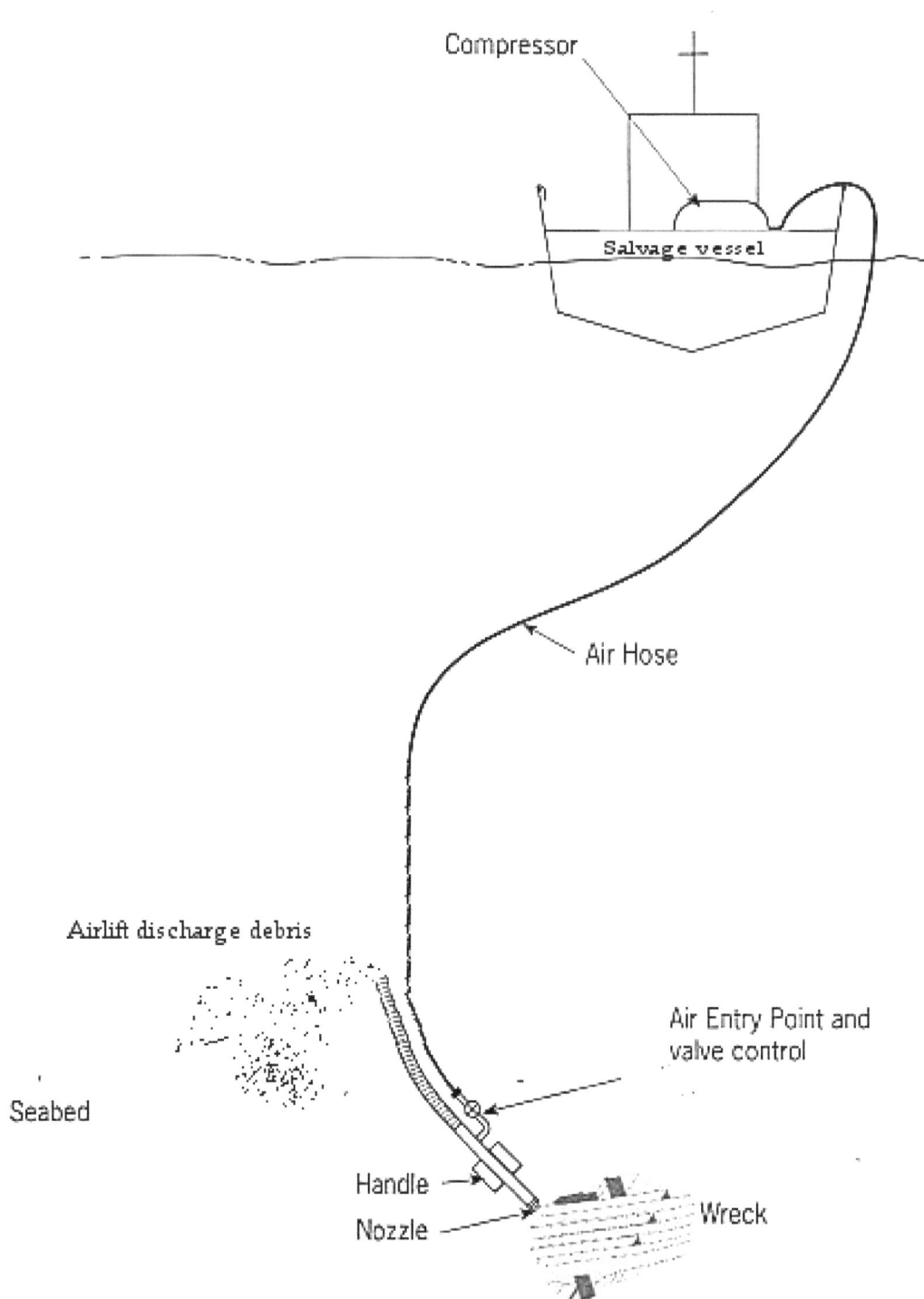

Compressor

Salvage vessel

Air Hose

Airlift discharge debris

Air Entry Point and valve control

Seabed

Handle

Nozzle

Wreck

Simple airlift with discharge back into the ocean. Generally requires two or three divers to utilize in a salvage operation where artifacts are being uncovered. Limited to an environment with at least some visibility to be effective.

Drawing by Jennifer Gunn ©WUAG- used with permission by Ed Cumming

(modified by author)

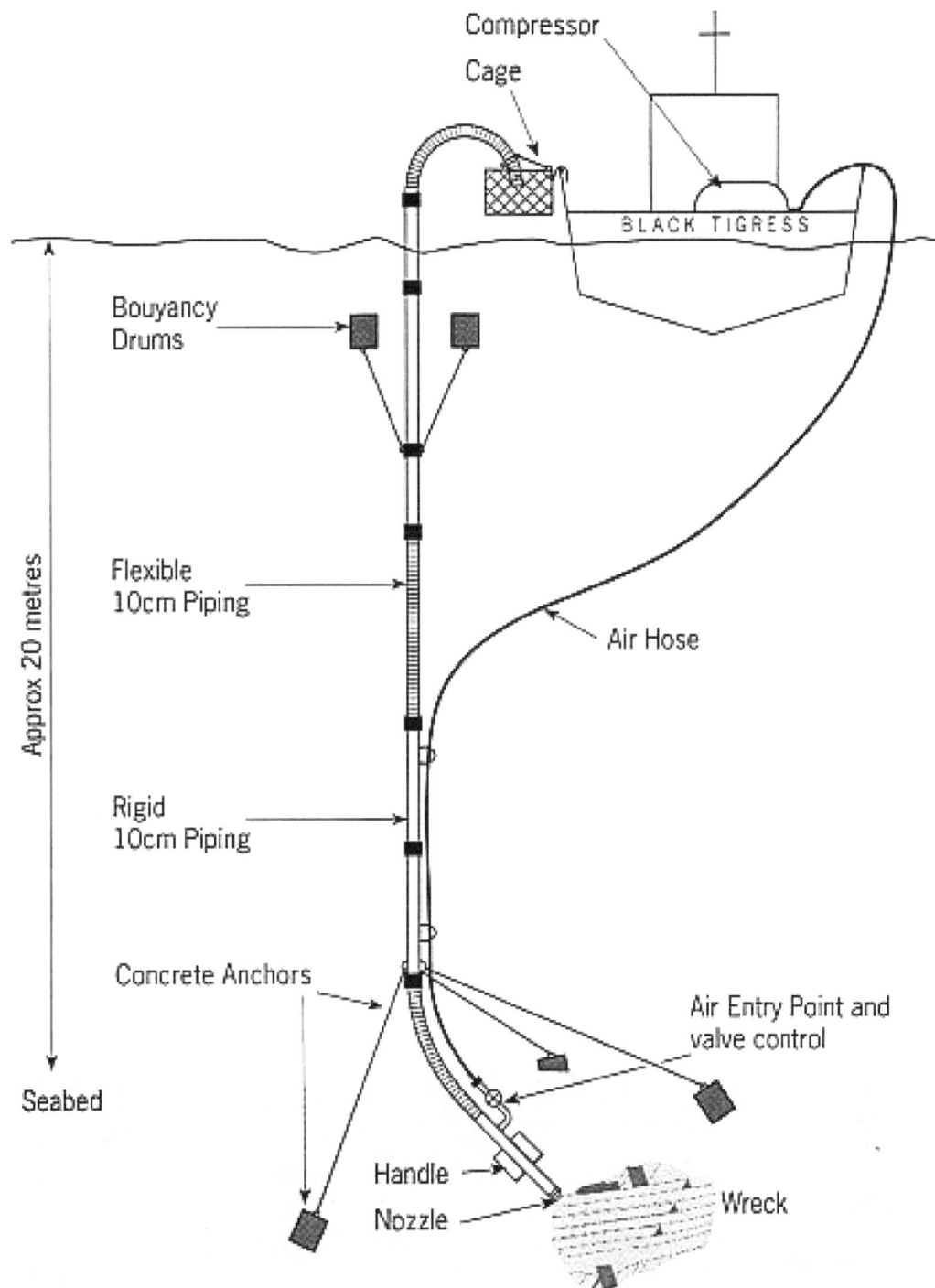

Compressor

Cage

BLACK TIGRESS

Bouyancy
Drums

Flexible
10cm Piping

Air Hose

Approx 20 metres

Rigid
10cm Piping

Concrete Anchors

Air Entry Point and
valve control

Seabed

Handle

Nozzle

Wreck

More complicated airlift which discharges above water, usually into a basket or onto an examination table where trained screeners look through what is being "vacuumed" off the bottom.

Drawing by Jennifer Gunn ©WUAG – used with permission by Ed Cumming

Dredges

The hydrolift, also called gold dredge, dredge, and transfer tube, works on the same principle as an airlift, except that water pressure and the "Venturi Effect" is used instead of air pressure. The tube is rarely more than six feet long and instead of discharging the spill on the surface it discharges it close behind the diver. We found the following article about dredges to be very informative and based on experience and facts. It is reproduced here with permission of the author, Ed Cumming.

****

THE PRINCIPLE AND DESIGN OF A WATER DREDGE

ED CUMMING

THE WATER DREDGE

There are two common techniques for the removal of overburden and excavation of wreck sites; the airlift and the water dredge. The principle of the airlift is probably the best understood and an article detailing the construction and operation of one particular design was the subject of an article in Diver April 1982, Vol. 24, No.4. This section will hopefully give divers a better understanding of the principles, construction and use of the dredge, and attempts to highlight any advantages or disadvantages when it is compared to the airlift.

PRINCIPLES & CONSTRUCTION

The water dredge being loaded on the dive boat.

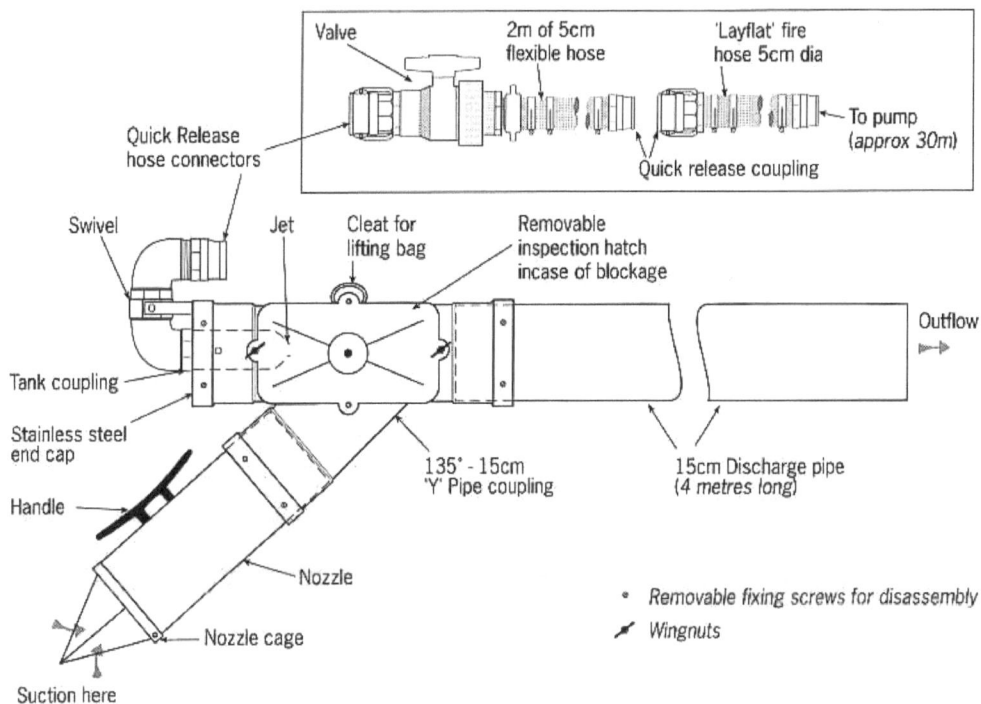

Valve

2m of 5cm
flexible hose

'Layflat' fire
hose 5cm dia

Quick Release
hose connectors

To pump
(approx 30m)

Quick release coupling

Swivel

Jet

Cleat for
lifting bag

Removable
inspection hatch
incase of blockage

Outflow

Tank coupling

Stainless steel
end cap

Handle

135° - 15cm
'Y' Pipe coupling

15cm Discharge pipe
(4 metres long)

Nozzle

Nozzle cage

Suction here

• Removable fixing screws for disassembly
⚲ Wingnuts

C.U.A.U. WATER DREDGE

J.A.Gunn © C.U.A.U.

Schematic of the water dredge.

A dredge is shown schematically in Figure 1 above and can be constructed very simply using plastic drainpipe and fittings (100-150 mm diameter are the most practical). Design features like the 50mm swivel coupling, which avoids problems with the hose kinking on the seabed, and the inspection hatch on the side of the 'Y' section drainpipe are not essential, but make the basic design easier to use and maintain underwater.

Unlike the airlift which uses air (and Boyles law) as its power source, the dredge uses a combination of water pressure and water flow from a powerful water pump to create the necessary suction at the nozzle. Many people consider that the dredge is only a shallow water device, this is not the case, they can be used very effectively at 30 metres. There is no need to worry about the pressure to be overcome at the working depth as is the case with the air supply to the airlift. The water pressure at any depth is proportional to the weight of an imaginary 'column' of water above, plus atmospheric pressure. Since the hose merely contains this 'column' the pump does not have to do any extra work in pumping on the surface or underwater to 30 metres. Flow losses do occur due to resistance as the hose length is increased; these losses are generally acceptable however.

The water enters the dredge via the supply hose and control valve (optional) to a jet fixed in a blanking plate mounted in the blind arm of the 'Y' pipe coupling. The jet, made from suitable copper pipe and fittings, must have a smaller cross-section than the supply hose so that pressure builds up behind it, directing pressurised water down the centreline of the discharge tube. The increased velocity and flow of water at the jet, commonly known as the 'Venturi' effect, creates a suction at the nozzle. An example of dredge head construction is shown in Figures 3 to 6.

This nozzle assembly is fitted with a swivel. Since the strain of the hose is taken here, the jet mounting plate was made of stainless steel.

Left - Swivel and jet mounted into the 'Y-section' drain coupling. Note the inspection hatch. Right - The completed swivel version of our dredge head complete with the inspection hatch cover. The cover bolts were modified to allow easy access without the need of a spanner.

Providing the pump is powerful enough and power losses are kept to a minimum, a well designed dredge will suck up almost similar quantities of material to a comparable diameter airlift. The only thing it will not do is bring the material to the boat unless the water is very shallow.

ANCILLARY EQUIPMENT

The major items are the pump and the hose. Correct choice of water pump is essential if the optimum performance is to be obtained from the dredge. Flow rate is major consideration but equally critical is the head pressure which is maintained behind the jet at the designed flow rate. Figure 7 shows the performance of the 50mm ALCON Pump which is one of the more use to power our 150 mm diameter dredge. It can be seen that the petrol engine option provides a significant increase in pump performance when compared with the diesel version. Figure 7 also shows the effect of suction height (or suction head) and the need to keep the pump as near to the waterline as possible. It will not matter if the intake hose has to rise over the gunwale or inflatable tube and then back down to the pump inlet since the rise and fall cancel out. It is the pump which must be as low as possible. 75mm pumps having similar or higher flow rates to the 50mm versions often develop lower head pressures and are not always as effective for dredge use. For short term projects, pump hire is probably the most cost effective; however these pumps are relatively cheap at £700 to £900 and for longer term use it may be worth buying one. If purchase is considered it is worthwhile stripping the pump and applying extra paint and/or corrosion inhibitor while new to give added protection. The pump must be cleaned thoroughly after each use, especially when used in salt water. Salt water resistant pumps are available but these tend to be more expensive and still require regular cleaning because the engine which drives the pump is unlikely to be protected.

The ideal hose is the 'lay flat' or 'fire' type since this will roll up neatly and take up little space. 15 metres of hose plus couplings will roll up into a coil about half a metre diameter. You will need a length at least twice the working depth and fittings to suit the chosen pump.

PERFORMANCE

The performance of any dredge will depend on many factors, the principal ones are as follows:-

- Flow rate of the pump.

- Head pressure of the pump.

- Power losses in the hose and couplings.

- Diameter of the 'venturi' jet.

- Diameter of the main dredge pipe.

- Length of discharge pipe.

- Angle of discharge pipe.

All these factors are interactive and it is therefore very difficult to give precise performance data for any particular size of dredge. It is generally a matter of 'suck it and see (sorry about that), however the table below gives a guide to the requirements and dimensions with an 'estimate' of performance.

Main Pipe Bore – millimeters	Jet Diameter - millimetres	Pump Output - litres/minute	Material Removed - cu. metres/hr
75	25	300 to 600	3
100	30	500 to 800	3 to 5
150	35	800 to 1200	6 to 8
200	50 to 60	2000 to 2500	?

OPERATION

The dredge is normally used in a horizontal attitude i.e., laying across the seabed, unlike the airlift which must be nearer to the vertical. It can be operated at a small angle and, in fact, dredges are used to bring material to the surface from shallow lakes and rivers. Too steep an angle or too long a discharge pipe however, causes loss of power and consequent blockage. The major advantages of the dredge technique are, in my opinion, the small size of the power source, i.e. the water pump, and the fact that the discharge tube need only be 2-3 metres in length. All the equipment necessary to operate a 150 mm unit can be comfortably carried in a 5 metre inflatable. It is worth remembering that a similar diameter airlift requires a small road compressor weighing about 700 Kg., whereas the ALCON 800 litre/minute pump weighs a mere 60 *Kg.,* and measures 50 cm x 50 cm x 40 cm.

This alternative dredge head without a swivel (shown at right), has a take off for a pressure jet, which is another very useful excavation tool.

Handling the dredge is in many ways similar to the airlift. The lay flat hose however needs careful handling to avoid any kinks; ideally keep it neatly coiled on a drum and once the dredge is attached, pay it out carefully from the boat as the diver descends to the site.

Anchoring the dredge needs careful thought so as to allow adjustment for manoeuvrability and also allow collection of the spoil in a small area for subsequent investigation of 'losses'. (Remember that the exit of the discharge tube must be positioned carefully to throw the spoil clear of the site and, of course, down tide.) Some excavators fit sieving systems to the discharge tube on the seabed and bring the contents to the surface for inspection. Operation in a strong tide is difficult and will be impossible without rigid anchoring points, (found from bitter experience) since the force of water acting on the cross section of several metres of delivery hose can be considerable. To overcome the problem, the delivery hose should be clipped at intervals to a strong mooring line and a long section of hose allowed to lay on the seabed (hopefully out of the tide) to allow manoeuvrability of the dredge. Try and complete the preparation at slack water.

During dredging, nozzle suction can be reduced by means of a valve (see Figure 1) but it is preferable to move the nozzle away from the work area since flow reduction in the discharge tube can cause blockages. Unless it is a matter of clearing overburden, manoeuvre the nozzle to allow objects to be found before they are sucked up.

In conclusion then, the choice of techniques, airlift versus dredge, will ultimately depend on the location of the site, longevity of the project and probably funds, since airlifting generally requires a much larger boat, and compressors are expensive. This article I hope, will enable divers contemplating underwater excavation, to consider the pros and cons of both these techniques and in the case of the dredge, build effective and robust equipment.

****

Water Jet/Air Jet

A **water jet**, which consists of nothing more than a hose blowing water out at high pressure, and an **air jet**, which operates on the same principle, are both useful as tools to blow away sediment under a ship's timbers, in ballast piles, or small sand pockets in coral reefs.

Metal Detectors

Metal detectors (handheld and towed) are used extensively in shipwreck salvage. There are several common technologies used in metal detectors, but that most often utilized in underwater metal detectors is *Pulse Induction.* In simple terms, the pulse induction machine simply fires a pulse of electromagnetic energy into the area around the coil. In the absence of metal, the 'spike' of energy decays at a uniform rate, and the time it takes to fall to zero volts can be accurately measured. However, if metal is present when the machine fires the pulse, a small current will flow from the metal, and the time for the voltage to drop to zero will be increased. These time differences are very small, but modern electronics make it possible to measure them accurately and identify the presence of metal at a reasonable distance.

Pulse Induction detectors have one major advantage over other metal detector technologies: they are virtually impervious to the effects of mineralization, and small objects such as rings and coins can be located even under highly-mineralized 'black sand'. They do have one disadvantage, which is that the currently available technology lacks the ability to incorporate much discrimination into a Pulse induction detector. So, they detect everything made of metal. This is usually not a problem when salvaging a shipwreck, since virtually everything is "treasure". Metal detectors have an advantage over magnetometers in that they can detect virtually any metal object, whereas magnetometers can only detect ferrous metals.

Pulse induction detectors come in a variety of sizes and shapes. Several manufacturers make large coils (36 inches to 48 inches) which are towed behind a boat. The primary limitation of a Pulse Induction metal detector is the distance from the coil at which an object can be detected. With a normal 8-inch or 10-inch loop, a large silver coin can be detected between 12 and 18 inches under the sand. With a larger loop, objects such as cannon or anchors may be detected up to several meters under the sand or sediment.

With these limitations, metal detectors are primarily used during the salvage phase of an operation, although the larger, towed units are used to pinpoint non-ferrous objects (bronze cannon, large silver bars, etc.) in an area where a shipwreck has been widely scattered by the elements.

The two images at the right show an Aquapulse AQ1B-Compact Pulse Induction underwater metal detector (top), and a JW Fisher Pulse 8X underwater metal detector (also Pulse Induction). Both of these units are favorites for the serious underwater treasure hunter/finder.

IDENTIFYING SHIPWRECKS FROM RECOVERIES

In this section we first discuss what a shipwreck is and what causes them. Then we present various artifacts commonly found on shipwrecks that are used to identify both the origin and age of a shipwreck. We found that many well-accepted assumptions are totally wrong. Most of this section applies to identification of shipwrecks between 1500 and 1900. We have also included a few less common artifacts, which proved a challenge to identify.

SHIPWRECKS – WHAT AND WHY?

What is a shipwreck and what causes them

A **shipwreck** is the remains of a ship that has wrecked, either sunk or beached. A shipwreck can refer to a wrecked ship or to the event that caused the wreck, such as the striking of something that causes the ship to sink, the stranding of the ship on rocks, land or shoal, or the destruction of the ship at sea by violent weather. Whatever the cause, a sunken ship or a wrecked ship is a physical example of the event. There are more than 3 million shipwrecks on the ocean floor, the United Nations estimates.

Design and equipment failure

At times ships sank due to poor design by being to narrow, having to little ballast area, and having the lower cannon deck with too low of a free board for good seaworthiness. Leaks between the hull planks of wooden vessels were a particular problem. Broken sails, failure of pumps, rudders, steering equipment, or engines, can all lead to disaster.

Instability

This can lead to a sinking if the openings on the upper side are not watertight at the time of a capsize. To remain buoyant, the hull of a vessel must prevent water entering the large air spaces of the vessel (known as down flooding). Clearly for the ship to float, the submerged parts of the hull will be watertight, but the upper parts of the hull must have openings to allow ventilation to compartments, including the engine room, for crew access, and to load and unload cargo.

Fire

Fire can cause the loss of ships in many ways.

In old ships, lighting was a hazard and caused many ships their end. Stoves on ships were another reason ships burned, the crew had to eat so they had to be able to cook.

The detonation of cargo or ammunition can cause the breach of a steel hull by causing the hull to break on its own weight. Often a large fire causes a ship to be abandoned and left to drift. Should it run aground beyond economic salvage, it becomes a wreck.

Bad weather

Poor weather can cause several problems:

- Wind
- Low visibility
- Cold

Wind causes waves, which result in other difficulties. Waves make navigation difficult and dangerous near shallow water. Also, waves create buoyancy stresses on the structure of a hull. The weight of breaking waves on the fabric of the ship force the crew to reduce speed or even travel in the same direction as the waves to prevent damage. Also, wind stresses the rigging of sailing ships.

The force of the wind pushes ships in the direction of the wind. Vessels with large windage suffer most. Although powered ships are able to resist the force of the wind, sailing vessels have few defenses against strong wind.

Many losses of sailing ships were caused by sailing, with a following wind, so far into a bay that the ship became trapped upwind of a lee shore, being unable to sail into the wind to leave the bay.

Low visibility caused by fog, mist and heavy rain increase the navigator's problems.

Cold can cause metal to become brittle and fail more easily. A build-up of ice can cause instability by accumulating high on the ship, or in severe cases, crush the hull if the ship becomes trapped in a freezing sea.

Construction materials

Exposed wooden components decay quickly. Bacteria and sea worms cause the ships hull to have leaks more rapidly in salt water. Steel and iron, depending on their thickness, may retain the ship's structure for decades. But, as corrosion eventually takes place, sometimes helped by tides and weather, the structure collapses.

Warfare, Piracy, Mutiny, or Sabotage

Many historical shipwrecks were the result of naval combat between ships of different countries, or between pirates and ships of any country.

Navigation errors

Many shipwrecks have occurred when the crew of the ship allowed the ship to collide with rocks, reefs, icebergs, or other ships. Collision has always been one of the major causes of shipwreck. Accurate navigation is made more difficult by poor visibility in bad weather. Also, many losses happened before modern navigation aids such as GPS, radar and sonar were available. Until the twentieth century, the most sophisticated navigational tools and techniques available - dead reckoning using the magnetic compass, marine chronometer (to calculate longitude) and ships logbook (which recorded the vessel's heading and the speed measured by log) or celestial navigation using marine chronometer and sextant - were sufficiently accurate for journeys across oceans, but these techniques (and in many cases also the charts) lacked the precision to avoid reefs close to shore. The Scilly naval disaster of 1707, which claimed nearly 2,000 lives and was one of the greatest maritime disasters in the history of the British Isles, is attributed to the mariner's inability to find their longitude. This led to the Longitude Act to improve the aids available for navigation. Marine chronometers were as revolutionary in the 19th century as GPS is today. However the cost of these instruments could be prohibitive, sometimes resulting in tragic consequences for ships that were still unable to determine their longitude.

Even today, when highly accurate navigational equipment is readily available and universally used, there is still scope for error. Using the incorrect datum for the chart of an area may mislead the navigator, especially as many charts have not been updated to use modern data. It is also important for the navigator to appreciate that charts may be significantly in error, especially on less frequented coasts. For example, a recent revision of the map of South Georgia in the South Atlantic showed that previous maps were in some places in error by several kilometers.

Over the centuries, many technological and organizational developments have been used to reduce accidents at sea including:

- International Regulations for Preventing Collisions at Sea
- Pilotage aids including lighthouses and sea marks
- Basic navigation tools such as the magnetic compass, nautical chart, marine chronometer, sextant, log and sounding line
- Advanced navigation tools such as radio communication, radar navigation, gyrocompass, sonar, hyperbolic Radio navigation and satellite navigation
- Inspection of shipbuilding quality and maintenance of seaworthiness of the ship such as "A1 at Lloyd's"
- Intelligence and better defenses to protect the ship from acts of violence, war and piracy

- Use of fireproof/nonflammable materials to prevent fires from spreading rapidly, and modern fire-fighting agents such as gases and foams that do not compromise the buoyancy and stability of the vessel as quickly as water.

- Built-in devices to delay flooding long enough for rescue ships to retrieve survivors and/or tow the ship to the nearest shipyard for repairs, such as watertight compartments and pumps.

ARTIFACTS FOUND ON SHIPWRECKS

General Discussion

Just because an artifact recovered from a shipwreck is from China does not mean the ship is Chinese, nor does it mean the ship originated from China on its final voyage. Trade goods were transported from many areas of the world and ended up on ships in the Caribbean headed for Spain in the Colonial times. The following discussion of the Manila Galleons helps shed some light on the wide variety of commodities that may be found on shipwrecks from this era.

Manila Galleons

The Manila galleons or Manila-Acapulco galleons (Spanish: *Galeones de Manila-Acapulco*) were Spanish trading ships that sailed once or twice per year across the Pacific Ocean between Manila in the Philippines, and Acapulco, New Spain (present-day Mexico). The name changed reflecting the city that the ship was sailing from. Service was inaugurated in 1565 with the discovery of the ocean passage by Andrés de Urdaneta, and continued until 1815 when the Mexican War of Independence put a permanent stop to the galleon trade route.

Though service was not inaugurated until almost 50 years after the death of Christopher Columbus, the Manila galleons constitute the fulfillment of Columbus' dream of sailing west to go east to bring the riches of the Indies to Spain, and the rest of Europe.

Trade served as the fundamental income-generating business for Spanish colonists living in the Philippine Islands. A total of 110 Manila galleons set sail in the 250 years of the Manila-Acapulco galleon trade (1565 to 1815). Until 1593, three or more ships would set sail annually from each port. The Manila trade was becoming so lucrative that Seville merchants petitioned King Philip II of Spain of their losses, and secured a law in 1593 that set a limit of only two ships sailing each year from either port, with one kept in reserve in Acapulco and one in Manila. An "armada", an armed escort, was also allowed.

With such limitations it was essential to build the largest possible galleons, which were the largest class of ships known to have been built anywhere up to that time. In the 16th century, they averaged from 1,700 to 2,000 tons, were built of Philippine hardwoods and could carry a thousand passengers. The *Concepción*, wrecked in 1638, was 43 to 49 m (140–160 feet) long and displacing some 2,000 tons. The *Santísima Trinidad* was 51.5 m long. Most of the ships were built in the Philippines and only eight in Mexico. The Manila-Acapulco galleon trade ended when Mexico gained independence from Spain in 1821, after which the Spanish crown took direct control of the Philippines. (This became manageable in the mid-1800s upon the invention of steam powered ships and the opening of the Suez Canal, which reduced the travel time from Spain to the Philippines to 40 days.)

The Manila-Acapulco trade route started in 1568 and was the rival of the Portuguese east trade routes of 1498-1640. The galleons carried spices, porcelain, ivory, lacquerware, processed silk cloth gathered from both the Spice Islands, and Asia-Pacific, to be sold in European markets. East Asia trading was primarily on a silver standard; the goods were mostly bought with Mexican silver. The cargoes were transported by land across Mexico to the port of Veracruz on the Gulf of Mexico, where they were loaded onto the Spanish treasure fleet bound for Spain. This route was the alternative to the trip west across the Indian Ocean, and around the Cape of Good Hope, which was reserved for Portugal according to the Treaty of Tordesillas. It also avoided stopping over at ports controlled by competing powers, such as Portugal and the Netherlands. From the early days of exploration, the Spanish knew that the American continent was much narrower across the Panamanian isthmus than across Mexico. They tried to establish a regular land crossing there, but the thick jungle, and malaria made it impractical.

It took four months to sail across the Pacific Ocean from Manila to Acapulco, and the galleons were the main link between the Philippines and the viceregal capital at Mexico City and thence to Spain itself. Many of the so-called "Kastilas" or Spaniards in the Philippines were actually of Mexican descent, and the Hispanic culture of the Philippines is somewhat close to Mexican culture. Even when Mexico finally gained its independence, the two nations still continued to trade, except for a brief lull during the Spanish-American War. The Manila galleons sailed the Pacific for nearly three centuries, bringing to Spain their cargoes of luxury goods, economic benefits, and cultural exchange.

The wrecks of the Manila galleons are legends second only to the wrecks of treasure ships in the Caribbean. In 1568, Miguel López de Legazpi's own ship, the *San Pablo* (300 tons), was the first Manila galleon to be wrecked en route to Mexico.

DID YOU KNOW?

- Its all about common sense

Coins

Of course coins, especially those with dates, can be very helpful in dating a shipwreck, and often in determining its origin. If you find a coin dated 1690 on a shipwreck, you know it definitely didn't sink BEFORE 1690. Some ships were carrying newly minted coins, so you will find many coins with the same date. This is very useful in dating the wreck and also in determining the name of the ship itself since good records were usually kept about mint shipments of coins and treasure.

There are two main types of coins found on shipwrecks from the 1500's through the 1800's, Cob coins and Milled coins. Cob coins are coins that were produced manually and no two are alike. These were produced from copper and copper alloys, silver, and gold. In the 1700's coins began to be produced with more modern equipment and the results were fairly uniform, round coins, usually with some kind of edge finish to discourage shaving the precious metal from the edge of the coin as was commonly done with the cob coins.

Cob coins were produced in vast quantities in the New World in various mints, as well as in Spain and its possessions. The images below show the most common silver coins found on Spanish shipwrecks from the 1600's -1800's.

Cob Shield Design Bolivia   Cob Shield Design-Mexico   Cob Pillars & Waves Design

8 Reales "Pillar Dollars"   8 Reales "Bust Dollars"

Examples of Gold Cob Coins

DID YOU KNOW?
- Jade is one of the oldest forms of money in the world

Cannon

Cannon serves both as the singular and plural of the noun, although the plural *cannons* is also accepted in American English

Cannon found by local fisherman and sold to restaurant in Bavaro, Dominican Republic.

Cannon are another thing that can be misleading when trying to identify the origin and date of a wreck. When a ship sank, if it could be salvaged, they always tried to salvage the cannon and anchors since they were a very valuable and necessary commodity. If the salvaged cannon were better than the ones on the salvor's ship, then they may have been substituted for the original ones. In this case, the salvor's cannon might have been cast overboard on or near the wreck site, which will only confuse the issue more for modern day salvors.

With proper research, you should be able to determine the approximate age and origin of the cannon, but as explained above, that doesn't necessarily help identify or date the ship. See our Archaeological Worksheets in our Archaeology chapter for help in gathering the data to identify cannon. An 18th Century Bronze Cannon is shown to the right.

A local fisherman said this cannon was found on a wreck in Cabeza de Toro. Although very long and slender, this piece appears very similar to drawings of Bombardetas, which have been salvaged from several Spanish shipwrecks from the 1500's (see Bombardeta below)

The first thing you should do when encountering a cannon on a shipwreck site is determine if it is iron or bronze. How do you do that? Always carry a magnet with you. Also, the copper in bronze is toxic to marine organisms and bronze cannon will usually be relatively free of marine growth and usually green or dark brownish green in color. Iron cannon are usually heavily encrusted unless they have been buried under mud or sand. Bronze cannon require little in the way of conservation, while iron cannon require very extensive conservation. Do NOT take iron cannon from the water unless you have facilities ready to conserve them.

Types of Cannon

Swivel Gun

The small forged swivel cannon were called Versos. These Versos were carried on ships as late as the 18th century. A Swivel Gun was a small piece of ordnance, turning on a point or swivel. A typical swivel gun might measure 33 inches (90 cm) in overall length, with a bore diameter of 1¼ inches (3.5 cm). It would have fired ¾ pound balls and would be wedged in place to use for anti-personnel fire. Besides their main defensive weapon, the

swivel gun was used for signaling and salutes. (Swivel gun photo used with permission - ©
BrokenSphere / Wikimedia Commons)

Chase Gun

The chase guns, usually distinguished as bow chasers and stern chasers (or just chasers for
short) were cannon mounted in the bow or stern of a sailing ship. They were used to
attempt to slow down a ship either pursuing or being pursued, typically by damaging the
rigging and thereby causing the target to lose performance.

Pivot Gun

A pivot gun was a large gun mounted on a pivot or revolving carriage, so as to turn in any
direction. By 1812 the long gun on a pivot had reached the height in popularity in America.

Vase Cannon

A rare cannon known as a Vase Cannon is depicted
to the right. It was designed to shoot arrows. This
is a photo of a reconstruction of a bronze vase
cannon. Permission: CC-by-sa GFDL

"Thunder Mug" or Signal Cannon

These small cannon were used to signal other
ships, and some sources say they were also used to
test the gunpowder. They are found on many
shipwrecks. The photo to the right shows two
bronze "Thunder Mugs' recovered from the Santa
Maria de la Consolación along with some cob coins
salvaged from the same shipwreck. Photo courtesy
William K. Seliger.

Bombardeta

The *bombardetas* were breech-loaded like the versos, and required a separate powder
chamber to be wedged against the barrel tube in order to be fired.

Barrel tubes up to 11 feet in length have been found on Spanish shipwrecks from the
1500's. These guns were built much like wooden casks or kegs. Iron staves the length of the
barrel are placed edge to edge, forming a cylinder over which a series of hoops and sleeves
were wrapped around or driven over, giving the barrels a segmented appearance. These
reinforcement bands served to bind the staves, making the barrels stronger.

Similar guns, mounted in wooden cradle-like carriages, have been recovered from several 16th century shipwreck sites including: the *Villefranche* wreck of ca. 1516, the *Mary Rose*, wrecked 1545, and on the St. Johns Bahamas shipwreck. A bombardeta barrel was also recovered from the wrecked 1554 fleet near Padre Island, Texas

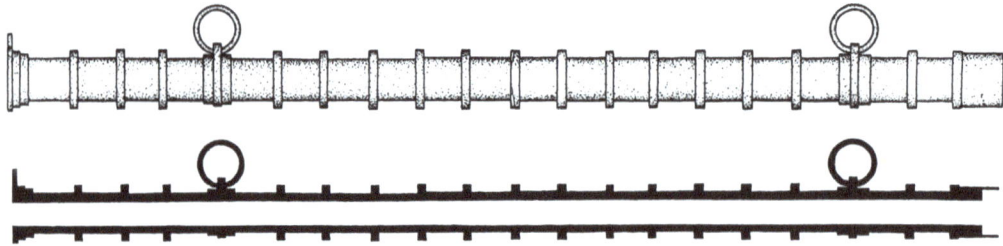

Bombardeta barrel tubes recovered from the St. John's Bahamas wreck – courtesy Mel Fisher Maritime Heritage Society, Inc.

Projectiles fired from cannon

Round shot or **solid shot** or a **cannonball** or simply **ball**

A solid spherical projectile made, in early times, from dressed stone but, by the 17th century, from iron. The most accurate projectile that could be fired by a smooth-bore cannon, used to batter the wooden hulls of opposing ships, forts, or fixed emplacements, and as a long-range anti-personnel weapon. Cannon balls are often found on older shipwreck sites, and are usually iron but may be found in bronze also. Iron cannon balls are usually very encrusted and deteriorate quickly if exposed to the air. Proper conservation is a must for iron cannon balls.

Photo at left shows various types of cannon balls found on the *Vasa*, the ones with bars and chains were specialty cannon balls for taking out ships rigging etc. – Photo courtesy Wikipedia. The photo at right shows a bronze cannon ball from the *Capitana* in Ecuador.

Chain shot or bar shot

Two sub-caliber round shot (a good deal smaller than the bore of the barrel) linked by a length of chain or a solid bar, and used to slash through the rigging and sails of an enemy ship so that it could no longer maneuver. It was inaccurate and only used at close range. **Two-headed bullets (angels)** were similar but made of two halves of a ball rather than two balls.

Canister shot

An anti-personnel projectile which included many small iron round shot or lead musket balls in a metal can, which broke up when fired, scattering the shot throughout the enemy personnel, like a large shotgun.

Shrapnel or spherical case shot

An iron anti-personnel projectile containing an interior cavity packed with lead or iron round balls around a small bursting charge of just enough force to break open the thin-walled iron projectile. A powder train in a thin iron sleeve led to a time fuse inserted into a holder at the outer edge or the projectile. The fuse was designed to be ignited by flame from the propellant charge. Ideally the case shot fuse would detonate the central bursting charge when the projectile was six to ten feet above the heads of enemy infantry thereby showering them with the iron balls and fragments of the casing. (Invented 1784 by Lt. Henry Shrapnel, Royal Artillery, Great Britain).

Shell

An explosive anti-material and counter-battery projectile, of iron with a cavity packed with a high explosive bursting charge of powder used to destroy enemy wagons, breastworks, or opposing artillery. Two types of fuses were used—impact fuses that detonated the bursting charge by percussion, and time fuse cut to length measured in seconds and ignited by flame from the propellant charge.[2]

Grapeshot

An anti-personnel weapon, similar to canister shot, but with the shot being contained in a canvas bag, and generally of a larger caliber, so called because of the resemblance of the clustered shot in the bag to a cluster of grapes on the vine. In one variation of this, the shot was held together by a coiled bar, and was spread by a fused charge in the same way as a shell. It was very effective against infantry, but its main shortcomings included very short range and ineffectiveness against infantry who had taken cover. Grapeshot was the starting point for the creation of shrapnel.

Carcass

An incendiary/antipersonnel projectile designed to burn fiercely and produce poisonous fumes. It was constructed of an iron frame bound with sack cloth and filled with various ingredients such as pitch, antimony, sulfur, saltpeter, tallow and venetian turpentine. It was ignited by the cannon's propellant charge, bursting on impact with the target and releasing noxious fumes while setting fire to its surroundings. It was effectively an early chemical weapon as well as an incendiary and area denial weapon. The name is possibly a reference to the medieval practice of hurling dead animals from trebuchet as a form of biological warfare, or to the projectile's superficial resemblance to a human carcass.

Heated (or hot) shot

A process where a solid iron cannonball is heated red hot in a specially-designed wood- or coal-fired furnace and then is loaded in a muzzle-loading cannon, cushioned by a substantial thickness of wet wads, and is then fired while still red hot, at flammable targets with the intention of setting them on fire. This was a much advocated tactic (and many times a very successful one) for shore based forts defending against attacks by wooden warships. Examples of these small brick furnaces may still be seen at permanently constructed pre-1860 forts in Europe and the United States. The adoption by most navies of iron hulled ships generally made these obsolete. The shot was carried on a specially-designed iron barrow or 2-man litter and, in the era of black powder cannon charges contained in cloth bags, occasioned much fanfare and notice as it was conveyed to the cannon muzzle as the red-hot projectile would easily ignite any carelessly handled loose powder. Any reckless or somewhat dangerous individual who seemed to draw trouble to themselves and those around them was referred to as a "Hot Shot", giving rise to the term in common use to this day.

Spider Shot

Spider shot is a chain shot, but it has many chains instead of just one. It was not often used, despite its effectiveness against small ships and morale.

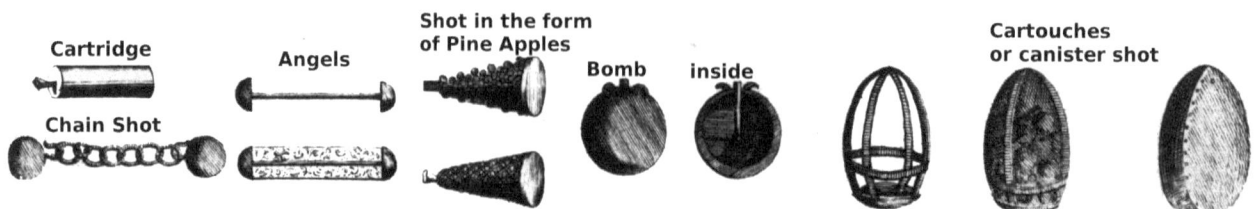

18th century cannon projectiles – courtesy Wikipedia

Some Cannon History and Facts

Eighteenth Century principal calibers and lengths of English cannon		
Caliber	Length of cannon in feet and inches	
	Bronze	Iron
3 lb	36"	4'6"
4 lb		6'0"
6 lb	4'4"	7'0" to 8'0"
9 lb	5'0"	7'0"
12 lb	5'6"	9'0"
18 lb	6'4"	9'0"
24 lb	7'0"	9'0" to 9'6"
32 lb	7'6"	9'6"
36 lb		
42 lb	8'4"	9'6" to 10'0"
48 lb	8'6"	

- The first confirmed use of gunpowder in Europe was the Moorish Gun (cannon), first used by the Andalusians in the Iberian Peninsula, at the siege of Seville in 1248, and the siege of Niebla in 1262

- The word cannon has been used to refer to a gun since 1326 in Italy, and 1418 in England.

- The Scots defended Stirling Castle with cannon in 1341, and Edward III used three cannon at the battle of Crécy-en-Ponthieu in 1346.

- Cannon were also used at Agincourt in 1415.

- By the mid-century there were so many sizes of cannon that they had to give them names in order to keep up with them. Henry II of France cut back to 6 six size's The Spanish had twelve size's the English had sixteen from 300 pounds to 4 tons.

- The earliest iron cannon were forged from iron strakes (strips) running the length of the barrel and held together by iron bands placed every 4 to 6 inches. In the 16th century these were called Lombard's.

- Later all cannon were made by pouring molten metal around a solid cylinder to form a chamber for powder and shot. Exact alignment was difficult and the interior cavity was often miss-shaped

- In 1740, Maritz of Switzerland made an outstanding contribution to the technique of ordnance manufacture. Instead of hollow casting (that is, forming the bore by casting the gun around a core), Maritz cast the gun solid, then drilled the bore, thus improving its uniformity. Metal impurities, known as slag, was forced to the center by the cooling action and removed by a lathe during the finishing operation.

- By 1750 design and construction were fairly well standardized in a gun of much cleaner line than the cannon of 1650.

- The solid-cast process came to America about 1773 and became standard practice for all U. S. cannon foundries. Sometimes it was necessary, to remove excess metal from the exterior to insure that the bore was accurately centered.

- Earlier pieces were rather flamboyant and bear fairly elaborate inscriptions and national emblems. Royal guns might bear the arms of the king for whom they were made, as well as those of the official -- his title varied from one country to another -- who supervised the manufacture of the king's cannon.

- Ordinance of this time might also bear mottoes and inscriptions identifying the gun-founder who cast the piece and the date it was made. In Earlier times English cannon, like others, were given names that indicated their sizes. Falcon, saker, demi-culverin, culverin, demi-cannon, cannon and basilisc described calibers from 2-1/2" up to 8-3/4", and weights from 800 lb up to 9000 lb.

- Many of the cannon had stamped on the trunnions, the manufacturer's mark

- The royal arms were replaced by a cipher, a crowned script monogram based on the initial of the king's name and these royal ciphers were done in Latin. Thus, "C VI R" stood for Carolus Sextus Rex - King Charles the Sixth.

- During Queen Elizabeth's time (1533-1603) came the 6-, 9-, 12-, 18-, 24-, 32-, and 42-pounder classifications adopted by Cromwell's government and used by the English well through the eighteenth century

- The French were acknowledged leaders. And King Louis XIV (1643-1715) brought several foreign guns into his ordnance, standardizing a set of calibers (4-, 8-, 12-, 16-, 24-, 32-, and 48-pounders) quite different from Henry II's in the previous century.

- In the 1700's cast-iron guns became the principal artillery afloat and ashore, yet cast bronze was superior in withstanding the stresses of firing. Iron reigned supreme until the advent of steel guns. But non-rusting bronze was always preferable aboard ship or in seacoast forts.

- When the supply of bronze was plentiful in Spain, the first class ships of the line were required to carry all bronze cannon. A royal order stated that all treasure galleons must carry all bronze cannon and that merchantmen must carry a minimum of two bronze pieces.

- It is interesting to note however, that by 1725 the use of bronze had faded and most of the cannon henceforth were iron.

- French cast-iron cannon had a touch hole that was drilled in a copper plug, which was hammered into the base of the cannon. The reason for this was probably to prevent stress concentrations that tended to burst cannon in this point when a small touch hole was used, but this is only a guess. The end of the bore was usually rounded out to a spherical shape to hold the charge.

- A peculiar type of cannon was the short-barreled mortar, named from its resemblance to a mortar for grinding. Early bombards were usually mortars. The first mortars appeared around 1420. The barrel was much shorter in terms of its diameter than that of the usual cannon, perhaps 8 calibers. The short barrel might occupy only about half the length of the piece,

Anchors

Anchors were generally made of iron, but there are documented cases of bronze anchors (see below), and a document attributed to Aristotle describes how Phoenician traders loaded so much silver on their ships that they even forged anchors made of silver.

According to *The Engineer's and Mechanics Encyclopaedia* by Luke Hebert, "Copper (bronze) anchors were sometimes made in Spain and the South Seas". We know that both copper and tin were abundant in South America during the Colonial period and many bronze items were fabricated there; while most iron objects were imported from Spain until the mid 1800's. Bronze cannon balls have been found on the *Capitana* shipwreck site in Ecuador.

The bronze anchor shown to the right is on display at a hotel in Higuey in the Dominican Republic. According to Bob Marx, he has found bronze anchors on several old wrecks over the years, all from 1500's-1600's and all quite large. He has a photo of his daughter standing by one from a Manila Galleon found off Monterrey, CA. He also found them on the *San Augustin* (also a Manila Galleon) lost in 1595 in Drake's Bay near San Francisco, which Bob found in 1950. There were 3 large bronze anchors on the *San Augustin*, one with a shank 26 feet long. Other than those, he claims he has seen TWO bronze anchors IDENTICAL to the one

in the photo to the right. These were on a 150 foot teak yacht of Haitian origin named the *Barracuda*. Bob was anchored behind a small island called Great Issac at the northwest corner of Great Bahama Bank, hiding from a Hurricane. The *Barracuda* came in, apparently to seek refuge from the Hurricane also. It anchored fairly close to Bob's boat and when Bob tried to make contact with the crew, they brandished weapons. During the night the crew of the *Barracuda* tried to board Bob's boat with automatic weapons. Fortunately Bob and his crew were watching for them and they were repelled. During the scuffle, the *Barracuda* cut their anchor lines and took off. The next day, Bob's crew dove up the *Barracuda's* abandoned anchors and the 500 feet of excellent nylon line attached, and recovered TWO Bronze anchors that Bob says were identical to the one on display in the hotel in Higuey

Anchors can be important clues, but they can also be virtually worthless in helping to find or identify a shipwreck. Anchors, like cannon, may have been acquired from other captured or salvaged ships. Because of their value and critical role, they were often the first thing salvaged from shipwrecks.

If a ship were at anchor when a storm came, the anchor line may have parted, leaving the anchor(s) where the ship had been anchored, while the ship may have wrecked many miles away; or many not have wrecked at all. Another scenario is where anchors were purposely cut loose and abandoned due to rapidly approaching bad weather, approaching enemy ships, or the anchor was hung up on something and the crew was unable to get it free. In these cases, the presence of the anchor means nothing except a ship anchored there.

Many shipwreck hunters state that the shank of an anchor will point towards the wreck site. That "may" be true, IF the ship were using anchor(s) to hold itself off a reef or offshore during a storm and the line(s) parted leaving it to the mercy of the winds and waves. In these cases, yes, the shank should be pointing more or less towards where the ship was being driven, and may lead you to the ultimate resting place. BUT, don't spend your lifetime looking in the direction of the shank; it may just be an abandoned or lost anchor as explained earlier.

The photo to the right is of an anchor near Boca de Yuma – courtesy Thomas Riffaud.

An example of anchors recovered from a wreck site and not conserved properly. These anchors were sold to a restaurant in Bavaro by a local fisherman. They are gradually disintegrating and, with the passage of time, will become ugly and be discarded. With proper conservation they would last several lifetimes.

Different types of Anchors

The Kedge Anchor

A Kedge Anchor, also known as "the fisherman" is the smallest of anchors and because of its light weight was used for calm weather and for moving up and down rivers. It was also used to pull a ship back out to deep water by taking the anchor in a small boat out to deeper water and pulling the ship to it, then lifting the anchor and doing it again. Not to be confused with the modern day light kedge anchor.

The Stream Anchor

The Stream Anchor is not much bigger than a Kedge Anchor and is for use in a river or sheltered place, where a small anchor is sufficient to hold the ship.

The Bow Anchors

The Bow Anchors or "Bowers" are for ordinary use and are stored at the bow, and if there is any difference in weight, the heavier is stored on the starboard side and is called the "Best Bower".

The Stern Anchor

The Stern Anchor is used to secure the stern of the ship when there is not room for the ship to swing with the tide.

The Sheet Anchors

The Sheet Anchors or "Waist Anchors" are the largest of the anchors and are stored as far forward as is convenient in the waist of the ship (hence the name "Waist Anchors") The Sheet Anchors are only used as a last resort to keep the ship from hitting a reef or shore, or if something befalls the Bow Anchors.

All anchors were made according to the ship's size so a Kedge Anchor of a very large ship could be the Sheet Anchor for a small ship.

Anchor Restoration and Preservation

Whole books are written about preserving recovered artifacts. We will briefly cover cannon and anchor preservation here, and deal with this subject in more depth in a future volume. Iron anchors and cannon recovered from the sea are often extensively damaged from exposure to salt water; because of this, electrolytic reduction treatment is required to forestall the process of corrosion. The object is then washed in de-ionized water to remove the electrolyte, and is treated in tannic acid, which prevents further rust and gives the metal a bluish-black color. After this process, anchors or cannon on display may be protected from oxygen and moisture by a wax sealant. A coat of polyurethane may also be painted over the wax sealant, to prevent the wax-coated artifact from attracting dust in outdoor displays.

Another example of what happens to anchors and cannon when they are not conserved properly. These were removed from the ocean by persons unknown and left to disintegrate on a public beach in Cabeza de Toro.

Interesting facts about anchors.

- In 1770 the iron cross stock was first used, but not until 1813 was the curved arm put into use by a clerk named Pering at the Plymouth Yard.
- In 1894 came the martin-Adelphi pattern that was a cast in one iron anchor.
- Early anchors were forged from one long piece of iron with one end split and both halves bent back to form the arms.
- Many anchors were probably lost in the deep because, at times, if a ship was threatened, it was more prudent to slip (leave) an anchor rather than delay leaving the area.
- It is also difficult to identify a shipwreck by its anchors, as anchors were a valuable commodity and ships would use salvaged anchors from any source.
- Large ships carried up to 9 or more anchors, and a 15-foot anchor could weigh as much as 5400 pounds. A 12-foot anchor would weigh about 2,800 pounds and a 9-foot anchor about 1,000 pounds.
- Ships that had 90-, 98-, 100-, or 110 guns had 7 Anchors.
- Ships from 20 to 80 guns carried 6 anchors.
- Ships of 300 tons and sloops had 5 anchors.
- Brigs and Cutters had 3 anchors.
- The Statutes of Genoa of 1441 AD required a 1500-ton ship to carry 12 iron anchors of from 1600 to 1800 pounds each.
- Most all anchor stocks were made of oak wood which almost always weighed 16-17 lbs per cubic foot. The anchor stock was also the same length as the anchor shank.
- Wooden stocks were used just about on every ship until the iron (cross) ones came out in the 1770's.
- Around 1775 the flukes or palms began to be cast in one piece with the arms.
- 1813 a clerk named Pering at the Plymouth Yard put the curved arm into use.
- In 1894 came the Martin-Adelphi pattern that was a cast-in-one iron anchor.
- Stockless Dansforth type anchors came into use in 1898.
- The figure to the right depicts the various types of anchor stocks in use circa 1794.

Traditional 2-piece Wooden Stock

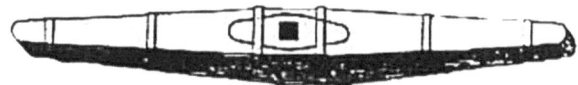

Lt. Rodgers' Wooden Stock

Admiralty Iron Stock

Lt. Rodgers' Iron Stock

Cotsell's Iron Stock

We have found that there is much misleading information about anchor weights. It depends on the year manufactured, country of origin, the thickness of the shank, etc. etc. So for this first edition of our book, we will go with the information below to have a general idea.

The weight of the Sheet Anchor (always the largest of the ship) was tied to the tonnage of the ship. For every 100 tons there would be 560 pounds of anchor weight for the Sheet Anchor.

Mr. Aubin, a 19th- century technician, states that the length of the anchor was 4/10th of the greatest breadth of the ship. In the 18th Century, William Sutherlands said that Royal Navy stipulated that the length of the shank of the ship's largest anchor was 2/5 of the widest point of the ship.

Length of Shank In feet and inches	Anchor weight In lbs.	Beam of Ship In Feet
3'2"	33	8
3'7"	47	9
4'0"	64	10
4'4	84	11
5'4"	175	14
6'0"	216	15
6'4"	262	16
6'10"	314	17
7'4"	373	18
7'7"	439	19
8'0"	512	20
8'5"	592	21
8'10"	681	22
9'2"	778	23
9'7"	884	24
10'0"	1000	25
10'5"	1124	26
10'10"	1259	27
11'2"	1405	28
11'7"	1562	29
12'0"	1728	30
12'5"	1906	31
12'10"	2097	32
13'2"	2300	33
13'7"	2515	34
14'0"	2742	35
14'5"	2986	36
14'10"	3242	37
15'2"	3515	38
15'7"	3796	39
16'0"	4096	40
16'5"	4426	41
16'10"	4742	42
17'2"	5088	43
17'7"	5451	44
18"	5832	45

Chains

Many treasure hunters and even archaeologists believe that if an iron chain is found on a shipwreck, it means it is from after the early 1800's. This is NOT the case. Chains were not common, but were used on ships beginning in the 1500's.

Interesting Chain Facts

- Prior to the use of chain, some of the anchor lines were as thick as 7" to 8" made of heavy Manila (hemp fiber). Can you imagine their weight when wet and the difficulty of retrieving the lines?
- In 1512 Chain was clearly depicted as being used on ships.
- In 1783 George Mathews of England made cast malleable chains for ships.
- In 1808 Englishman Robert Flinn of **B**ell St. North shields made the first improved iron chain which would become the standard for 100 years. (Reference: Baldt - Chester, Pa.)
- In the year 1831 chain cable began to supersede the hempen ones but chain was used as early as 1300 BC.
- In 1840 side welding of chain was introduced in England, and from that time English chains of 1-7/8 inches and larger have been side welded.
- In 1890 Lloyd's register rules set a table of minimum weights for cables.

Ship's Bells

- Bells have a centuries-long tradition of varied use in the navies and merchant fleets of the world. They have been used for signaling, keeping time, and providing alarm.

- Bells cast from metal were first developed in the Bronze Age, achieving a particularly high level of sophistication in China during the European Middle Ages.

- One of the earliest recorded mentions of the shipboard bell was on the British ship Grace Dieu about 1485. Some ten years later an inventory of the English ship Regent reveals that this ship carried two "watch bells".

- The sounding of a ship's bell found a natural application as a warning signal to other vessels in poor visibility and fog their most important modern use.

- Ringing a ship's bell in fog became customary. In 1858, British Naval Regulations made it mandatory in that function.

- The ship's cook (or his/her staff) traditionally has the job of shining the ship's bell.

- Strikes of a ship's bell are used to indicate the hour aboard a ship and thereby to regulate the sailors' duty watches.

- The term "Eight bells" can also be a way of saying that a sailor's watch is over, for instance, in his or her obituary. It's a nautical euphemism for "finished".

- The ship's name is traditionally engraved on the bell, often with the year the ship was launched as well. Occasionally (especially on more modern ships) the bell will also carry the name of the Ship Yard that built the ship.

- If a ship's name is changed, maritime tradition is that the original bell carrying the original name will remain with the vessel. A ship's bell is a prized possession when a ship is broken up, and often provides the positive means of identification a shipwreck.

Ships Ballast

Ships Ballast is (but not limited to) a heavy material, such as gravel, stone, sand, barrels of water or metal pigs iron and in some case's bricks, placed in the hold of a ship in order to immerse her sufficiently to give adequate stability to prevent her leaning over too easily when the wind blows against her side or sails.

Iron ballast

Melbourne Australia had over 40 local foundries that were kept busy, melting and casting pig-iron bars that arrived as ship's ballast in the mid 1800s. The photo below shows pig iron ballast at shipwreck site.

Stone ballast

Ballast stones used in Spanish ships constructed in South America and most Spanish shipwrecks found in the Caribbean and Atlantic waters normally have ballast stones from rivers with size's ranging from lemon-size to watermelon-size and larger. The photo to the right shows a ballast pile of small to medium size ballast stones.

This photo shows much larger ballast stones next to a pair of iron cannon.

Brick Ballast

The English used bricks for ships ballast on many occasions. Here are three documented examples:

- St. John's Cathedral is the oldest Anglican Church in Central America, and one of the oldest buildings in Belize. The orange bricks came to Belize aboard British ships as ballast. Construction began in 1812, and the church was completed in 1820.

- Another instance was at the church in Malaysia, Christ Church at Malacca. Upon reaching Malacca, the sailors would be ordered to unload the bricks to be used for construction there. The ballast was replaced with commercial merchandise for their continued journey, sailing either to Indonesia, to other Dutch colonies in Asia or back to the Netherlands.

- St. John's Anglican Cathedral. With its cornerstone laid in 1812 and consecration in 1826, it is the oldest Anglican Cathedral in Central America. The building was constructed of bricks brought from Europe as ballast in sailing ships, with labor provided by slaves!

Photo showing large pile of brick ballast

Ingots

Everyone's dream is to find a shipwreck full of gold or silver ingots. Although many shipwrecks have been found with large quantities of gold and silver in both ingots and coins, there are often other ingots to be found. It was common to ship tin, copper, and lead in the form of "splash ingots" in the early Colonial period. "Splash ingots" are ingots made by creating a depression in the earth and pouring the molten metal into the depression to cool. Needless to say, these ingots are usually quite contaminated with dirt and pebbles, and they are always misshapen and often very large – weighing well over 100 pounds. Tin is often found in formed ingots similar in size and shape (and of course color) to the large (60-80 pound) silver ingots we would all like to find. Official silver ingots will always have many markings on them, so if you don't see markings, it's either a contraband silver ingot or more likely a tin ingot. There are cheap acid test kits for testing for silver, but the only sure way to tell what you have is to get a sample assayed. Gold is often found in what are called "finger bars" (see photo below).

Copper, tin, and lead ingots found on a shipwreck

Silver bar (left) and gold "finger bar" (right)

Navigation Instruments

Although ancient navigational instruments are rarely found in good shape on shipwrecks, they are indeed found. Their presence can help date the shipwreck and most of them are prized discoveries in any condition. The Astrolabe is probably the instrument most likely to have survived since it was usually made totally of bronze, while the others often had wooden parts. The following early navigational instruments might be found on shipwrecks:

Mariner's Astrolabe

The "astrolabe" or "star-taker" -is an elaborate navigation tool and is said to be the first scientific instrument used for navigation. It is believed that the astrolabe originated in ancient Greece and was later "refined" by the Arabs into a more sophisticated device - highly artistic and ornamented. But the older and plainer astrolabe was the original tool. It was a disk with degrees of arc around its circumference and sight vanes on a rotating pointer called" alidade." The disk was most commonly made of brass and was vertically hung from a ring. The navigator would hold the device by that ring and raise it above his head. Then he would align the alidade, so that the star or planet he is measuring by could be seen in a straight line - through both pinhole sights in the sight vanes. The angle of this line of view was then read by the alidade and converted into latitude.

Quadrant

The quadrant is another instrument which seamen adapted for navigation. Its name comes from the quarter-circle that it uses as a scale. The simplest quadrants are made of a 90-degree protractor with a plumb weight hanging from its vertex.

Quintant

The quintant (not shown) was short-lived, less than two years by most accounts. The scale of a quintant has a length of 1/5 of a full circle (72°)

Octant

The octant (shown to the right) - the sextant's predecessor - was invented in 1730 in England and America, almost at the same time. In America Thomas Godfrey, associate of Benjamin Franklin, came up with the device. In Britain John Hadley made the discovery. The octant was a double-reflecting instrument using two mirrors.

Sextant

In the year 1731, the Sextant was invented by John Hadley. The sextant works on the same principle as the octant – superimposing the images of the two objects, the distance between which is measured. The sextant is an instrument used to measure the angular distance between two objects. By calculating the angular elevation of the sun or other celestial bodies, a navigator can determine both his longitude and his latitude

Cross-staff

The cross-staff is a tool that was used for centuries as an astronomers' tool before the German mathematician and navigator Martin Behaim adapted it for celestial navigation in the 1480s. The cross-staff, or Jacob's staff, was a long, square rosewood or ebony staff, and a shorter crosspiece (transom), which slides up and down the staff. The staff functioned in the following way: it was placed close to the eye and the crosspiece was adjusted so as "to fill the apparent distance between Polaris or the sun and the horizon. Then, by the position of the crosspiece on the staff, an angular measurement was taken on the scale on the edge of the staff.

Back-staff

The first navigational instrument, whose creator's name is known for sure, was the back-staff. An English explorer of the 16th century, John Davis, was impressed by the cross-staff, but wanted to improve upon it, to avoid the error due to the "disorderly placing of the staff to the eye." His 1590 device (also known as the Davis or English quadrant) was so simple and accurate that it earned a place in navigation for over 200 years. Though simple in its application, the device is hard to describe. In just a few words though: it was made up of three vanes (sight, shadow, and horizon) and a pair of arcs attached to a staff and divided in degrees. The sight vane slides along the sight arc just as the shadow vane slides along the shadow arc. The two arcs are part of two circles with a common center. That center is found on the horizon vane. The small arc measures 60 degrees and the large one - 30, thus providing a maximum zenith altitude of 90 degrees. In simpler terms, the back-staff was an improvement over the cross-staff, because it allowed the navigator to take the measurement standing with his back to the sun (hence the name) and using the sun's shadow. The glare from looking directly into the sun was thus avoided resulting in greater accuracy.

Ceramics

One of the most common ceramic artifacts found on shipwrecks between 1500 and the mid 1800's is the "olive jar". This is an earthenware jar that was manufactured in various sizes and shapes and used to transport everything from water, wine, and oil, to flour, sugar, and other foodstuffs. Most shipwrecks from this time period have large quantities of broken "olive jars" and usually some intact ones.

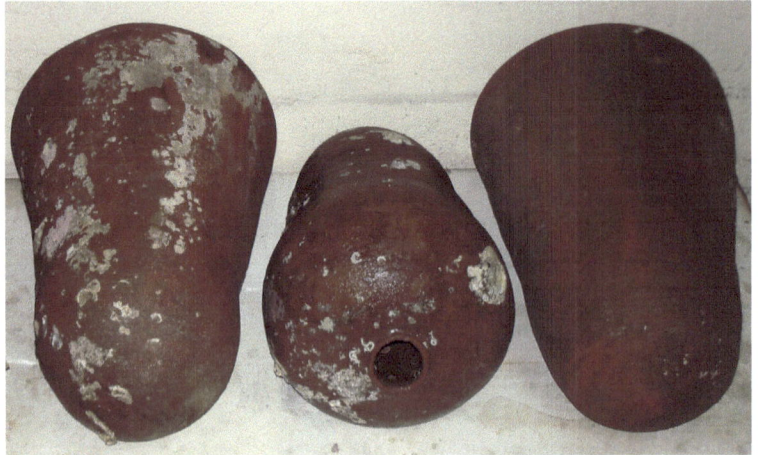

Ceramic "Olive Jar" shards from a wreck site

Other ceramics were also quite common on ships during this time period. Majolica plates, cups, saucers, pitchers, etc. were produced in Peru and other South and Central American countries and used widely on ships in the South Seas and Caribbean. Also, Asian ceramics and porcelain were introduced into the New World with the Manila Galleon traffic and many shipwrecks in the South Seas, the Caribbean, and the Atlantic have Chinese porcelain on them. Of course ships were often captured or salvaged after sinking and their "stuff" was often taken by the victor or salvor to replace or supplement their own. So nationality or origin of a ship is not so easily determined based on artifacts recovered.

Majolica plate (left) and cup and saucer (right) made in Peru found on a shipwreck

Chinese porcelain is also often found on Colonial shipwrecks from all countries

Timbers and wood

Another false assumption is that a wooden shipwreck in tropical waters will have no intact wood left if it is over 100 years old. This is a foolish assumption to make. There are many types of wood and some ships were built from wood that is virtually indestructible by immersion in water and is not attacked by any of the normal wood-destroying critters that inhabit the ocean. In addition, it depends greatly on the environment in which the shipwreck rests. Very cold water inhibits the growth of many marine organisms and Teredo worms don't seem to be as active in cold water as they are in warmer waters.

Some areas may be in what is considered a tropical climate, but very cold currents keep the water temperature low enough to inhibit the Teredo worms. Deep wrecks also have limited deterioration or damage from marine life, and anaerobic conditions inhibit or slow down the natural breakdown and deterioration of wood. If a wreck is buried under many meters of sand or is covered by deposits of mud or clay from a nearby river, the wood can be very well preserved even after hundreds of years.

This is the case for both the ships timbers and also other items made of wood, such as ships rigging, wooden chests, and even furniture.

Solid ships timbers on a 300+ year old shipwreck in the Pacific Ocean

Spikes, Nails, Tacks, and "Washers"

Another widely accepted belief is that shipwrecks can be dated based on round spikes vs square spikes, and bronze spikes vs iron spikes. This may be true to some extent, but both round and square bronze spikes date back to pre-Christian eras. The authors have seen wrecks from the 1600's with both iron and bronze spikes on the same wreck. Some of the larger bronze spikes have what appear to be large bronze "washers" on them and many believe this means the wreck is a newer wreck from the 1800's. But records from shipyards in the 1600's show diagrams with the "washers" being used in a fashion similar to a rivet. One end of the spike is flattened out like a head and a "washer" is placed on the spike and positioned against the "head". The spike is then placed through holes in the timbers to be joined and another "washer" is placed over the protruding end. The spike is then cut off a short distance past the "washer" and the short end is hammered down to make another "head" so it can't slide back through the "washer".

Copper and Lead Sheathing

There are also many misconceptions about dating a wreck based on whether or not it has copper sheathing or lead sheathing or no sheathing.

Throughout history, wooden ships and wooden docks and pilings have been plagued by damage from what is commonly known as Teredo Worms or Shipworms or "Termites of the Sea", as well as various other marine organisms. The Teredo worm is actually not a worm at all, but a mollusk that bores into the wood and digests the cellulose. To combat these damaging organisms, the ancient Phoenicians and Carthaginians were said to have used lead sheathing in 412 BC. The Greeks and Romans both independently used lead sheathing, which the Romans secured by copper nails. In the early 1500s, Spain officially adopted lead sheathing and its use soon spread to France and England. Although it actually offered little in the way of protection against fouling from marine growth, it did offer fairly reliable protection against the Teredo. Lead was the material most frequently used prior to the 1700s. However, its corrosive effect on the iron used in ships was soon noted, and the British Admiralty abandoned the use of lead in 1682 for this reason.

Other treatments to prevent worms from penetrating the planking relied on a wooden sheath placed over a layer of animal hair and tar. The wooden sheathing was sometimes filled with iron or copper nails with large heads, in effect creating an outer metallic cladding, or painted with mixtures of tar, brimstone and grease. In the 1600's copper sheathing was tried and found to be effective against the Teredo worms and also proved to be a very effective antifouling treatment. The first documented evidence for the use of copper as an antifouling is a patent dated 1625. The first authenticated use of copper was in 1758 on HMS Alarm, and by 1780 copper was in general use by the British Navy. Sir Humphrey Davy clearly showed that it was the dissolution of copper in seawater which prevented fouling, since when metallic copper was coupled to zinc or iron it failed to have an antifouling effect.

The antifouling properties of copper sheathing were so effective that many of the first iron ships were sheathed in copper. But it was found that the copper reacted badly with the iron causing severe damage to the ships, so the use of copper sheathing on these boats was discontinued.

So, although unlikely, it is possible you may find an iron shipwreck with copper sheathing. Run that one by your treasure hunting buddies and see how they react.

Other Artifacts

Here we present other artifacts that are commonly found on shipwrecks and can help identify the wreck, the time period, and the country of origin and/or destination.

Lead Seals
Lead Seals were used to mark and secure merchandise. These can be useful in determining the content and origin of cargo.

Mortar and Pestle
Bronze Mortar and Pestle and other medical implements are often recovered from shipwreck sites. It is important to recognize them for what they are, and not think they are some modern contamination of the site.

Religious items

Various religious items are regularly found on shipwrecks from the Colonial period. Many of these are considered personal items, but often ships of that time were carrying cargo of religious items such as crucifixes, rosaries, and medals similar to the one shown here.

Strange "stuff"

Often salvors find items that defy identification, at least for a while. Here are a few.

"Seat of Ease"

This artifact is known as "the seat of ease". This flanged, tapered lead pipe in its original form was known to many as the ships' "head" or "latrine", which was the sanitary facility for everyone aboard the ship. For the crew and most officers, these individual sanitary facilities or "seats of ease" were located on each side of the ship's bow and equipped with drainage sluices to direct human refuse downward to the sea.

For the officers, these accommodations were located at the ship's stern in an area known as the quarter galleries. These galleries or balconies were projected from the stern area allowing drainage downward to the sea. Various tapered lead tubing labeled either 'pissdales' or 'seats of ease' have been recovered from various shipwrecks, Whydah (1717), Henrietta Maria (1700), and Dartmouth (1690), indicating these accommodations were available to the crew. The remains of the seat of ease's wooden portion have only been recorded on one shipwreck, *Vasa* (1628). Photo courtesy *Queen Anne's Revenge*.

Bronze Church Door Ornaments

Many bronze "star shaped" objects were found on the *Consolación* shipwreck and remained a mystery for many months. Finally someone visiting a Colonial era church in Quito recognized the objects decorating the outside of the massive wooden doors – still in use today – see photos before and after restoration. Photos courtesy William G. Seliger.

Copper Pot Handles

Although they look somewhat like the bronze *Manilla* "African Slave Money" (see photos), these copper artifacts, often found on Spanish Colonial shipwrecks, are actually the handles from large cooking pots. Usually the pot has corroded away leaving only the handles, or sometimes the handles attached to the rim of the pot. *Manilla* shown on left side and copper pot handle on the right.

Deck Prism

A Deck Prism is a prism inserted into the deck of a ship which provides light down below. Top photo shows a group of deck prisms of different sizes and shapes – courtesy Wikipedia. Bottom photo is a deck prism from an unknown shipwreck – courtesy Steve Hodges, West Bay Trading Co.

For centuries, sailing ships used Deck Prisms to provide a safe source of natural sunlight to illuminate areas below decks. Before electricity, light below a vessel's deck was provided by candles, oil and kerosene lamps - all dangerous aboard a wooden ship. The deck prism was a clever solution: laid flush into the deck, the glass prism refracted and dispersed natural light into the space below from a small deck opening without weakening the planks or becoming a fire hazard.

In normal usage, the prism hangs below the ceiling and disperses the light sideways; the top is flat and installed flush with the deck, becoming part of the deck. A plain flat glass would just form a single bright spot below-- not very useful general illumination-- hence the prismatic shape.

On colliers (coal ships), prisms were also used to keep check on the cargo hold; light from a fire would be collected by the prism and be made visible on the deck even in daylight.

The names "deck light", "dead light" or "deadlight" are sometimes used, though the latter is uncommon as a reference to prisms, as more often refers to non-opening plain-glass panels.

SHIPWRECKS AND THE LAW

(Courtesy: Wikipedia)

Shipwreck law determines important legal questions regarding wrecks, perhaps the most important question being the question of ownership. Legally wrecks are divided into *wreccum maris* (material washed ashore after a shipwreck) and *adventurae maris* (material still at sea); although some legal systems treat the two categories differently, others treat them the same.

Wrecks are often considered separately from their cargo. For example, in the English case of the *Lusitania* [1986] it was accepted that the remains of the vessel itself were owned by the insurance underwriters who had paid out on the vessel as a total loss by virtue of the law of subrogation (who subsequently sold their rights), but that the property aboard the wreck still belonged to its original owners (or their descendants).

Military wrecks, however, remain under the jurisdiction–and hence protection–of the government that lost the ship, or that government's successor. Hence, a German U-boat from World War II still technically belongs to the German government, even though the Third Reich is long-defunct. Many military wrecks are also protected by virtue of their being war graves.

However, many legal systems allow the rights of salvors to override the rights of the original owners of a wreck or its cargo. As a general rule, non-historic civilian shipwrecks are considered fair game for salvage. Under international maritime law, for shipwrecks of a certain age, the original owner may have lost all claim to the cargo. Anyone who finds the wreck can then file a salvage claim on it and place a lien on the vessel, and subsequently mount a salvage operation (Finders, keepers).

Some countries assert claims to all wrecks within their territorial waters, irrespective of the interest of the original owner or the salvor. Wartime wrecks have different legal considerations, as they are often considered prizes of war, and therefore owned by the Navy that sunk them.

Some legal systems regard a wreck (and/or its cargo) to be abandoned if no attempt is made to salvage them within a certain period of time. English law has usually resisted this notion (encouraged by an extremely large maritime insurance industry, which asserts claims in respect of shipwrecks which it has paid claims on), but is has been accepted to a greater or lesser degree in an Australian case and in a Norwegian case. The American courts have been inconsistent between states and at Federal level. Under Danish law, all shipwrecks over 150 years old belong to the state if no owner can be found. In Spain, wrecks vest in the state if not salvaged within 3 years. In Finland, all property on board shipwrecks over 100 years old vests in the state.

The British Protection of Wrecks Act, enacted to protect historic wrecks, controls access to wrecks such as Cattewater Wreck which can only be visited or investigated under license. The British Protection of Military Remains Act 1986 also restricts access to wrecks which are sensitive as war graves. The Protection of Military Remains Act in some cases creates a blanket ban on all diving; for other wrecks divers may visit provided they do not touch, interfere with or penetrate the wreck. In the United States, shipwrecks in state waters are regulated by the Abandoned Shipwrecks Act of 1987. This act is much more lenient in allowing more open access to the shipwrecks.

Following the beaching of the MSC *Napoli*, as a result of severe damage incurred during European windstorm Kyrill, there was confusion in the press and by the authorities about whether people could be prevented from helping themselves to the flotsam which was washed up on the beaches at Branscombe. Many people took advantage of the confusion and helped themselves to the cargo. This included many BMW motorbikes and empty wine casks as well as bags of disposable nappies (diapers). The legal position under the Merchant Shipping Act 1995 is that any such finds and recovery must be reported within 28 days to the Receiver of Wreck. Failure to do so is an offense under the Merchant Shipping Act and can result in a criminal record for theft by finding. After several days, the police and Receiver of Wreck, in conjunction with the landowner and the contracted salvors, established a cordon to prevent access to the beach. A similar situation occurred after the wreck of the MV *Cita* in 1997.

Historic wrecks (often but not always defined as being more than 50 years of age) are often protected from pillaging and looting through national laws protecting cultural heritage. Internationally they may be protected by a State ratifying the UNESCO Convention on the Protection of the Underwater Cultural Heritage. In this case pillaging is not allowed.

An important international convention aiming at the protection of underwater cultural heritage (including shipwrecks) is the **Convention on the Protection of the Underwater Cultural Heritage.** The 2001 UNESCO Convention on the Protection of the Underwater Cultural Heritage represents the international community's response to the increasing looting and destruction of underwater cultural heritage. It forms part of a group of UNESCO standard setting instruments regarding the domain of cultural heritage, encompassing seven conventions adopted by UNESCO Member States, which constitute a coherent and complementary body guaranteeing a complete protection of all forms of cultural heritage.

The UNESCO 2001 Convention is an international treaty aimed exclusively at the protection of underwater cultural heritage and the facilitation of international cooperation in this regard. It does not change sovereignty rights of States or regulate the ownership of wrecks or submerged ruins

SOURCES

Other

- BALDT, Inc.
  801 W. 6th Street
  Chester, PA 19013
  phone: 610-447-5200 fax: 610-874-8599
  chain@baldt.com

- British Museum Library, London

- Dr. Lee Spence

- ST. JOHN'S BAHAMAS SHIPWRECK PROJECT
  INTERIM REPORT I: THE EXCAVATION AND ARTIFACTS 1991-1995 Mel Fisher Maritime
  Heritage Society, Inc. Key West, Florida

- The Naval Historical Society of Australia, Inc., Mackenzie J. Gregory and Winslow
  Homer, 1887

Books

Bass, George F., *Underwater Archaeology*, 1966, NY
   Ships and Shipwrecks of the Americas: A History Based on Underwater Archaeology,
   1996, Thames and Hudson
Bouguer, Pierre Jean, *Traite de Navire*, 1746
Breeden, Robert L., Editor, *Undersea Treasures*, Special Publications Division, National
   Geographic Society, Washington D.C., 1974.
Brewington, M.V., *Navigating Instruments*, 1963, Salem, MA
Chaunu, Pierre, *Seville et l'Atlantique 1504-1650,* 11 vols., 1959, Paris
Deagan, Kathleen, *Artifacts of the Spanish Colonies of Florida and the Caribbean, 1500-
   1800, Volume 1: Ceramics, Glassware, and Beads*, 1987, Smithsonian Institution Press
   *Artifacts of the Spanish Colonies of Florida and the Caribbean, 1500-1800, Volume 2:
   Portable Personal Possessions,* 2002, Smithsonian Institution Press
de Latil, Pierre and Jean Rivoire, *Sunken Treasure*, Hill and Wang, New York, 1962
Fike, Richard F., *The Bottle Book – A Comprehensive Guide to Historic Embossed Medicine
   Bottles*, 1987

Fincham, John, *A History of Naval Architecture*, 1851, London

Herbert, Luke, *The Engineer's and Mechanics Encyclopaedia*, 1836, London

Hogg, O.F.G., (Oliver Frederick Gillilan), *English Artillery 1326-1716,* 1963, London

Howse, Derek & Thrower, Norman J. W., *A Buccaneer's Atlas*, 1992, University of CA

Jamieson, Ross W., *Majolica in the Early Colonial Andes: The Role of Panamanian Wares.* In *Latin American Antiquity,* 2001

Johnstone, Paul, *The Archaeology of Ships*, 1974, London

Kordac, Dr. Lubos, *Historic Shipwrecks Of The Dominican Republic And Haiti*, 2009

Mainwaring, Sir Henry, *The Seaman's Dictionary*, (c.1624)

Manucy, Albert, *Artillery Through the Ages*, 1949, Washington, D.C.

Marx, Robert F., *Shipwrecks of the Western Hemisphere 1492-1825,* 1971, NY *Shipwrecks in the Americas*, 1987, Dover Publications

McCarthy, Michael, *Ships Fastenings*, 2005, Texas A&M University Press

Pering, Richard, *A Treatise on the Anchor (1819),* 2009, Whitefish, MT

Rider, Dennis, *A History of Glass Bottles*, 1956, London

Sedwick, Daniel and Frank, *The Practical Book of Cobs, 4th Edition*, 2007, Winter Park, FL

Shepard, Anno O., *Ceramics for the Archaeologist*, 1965, Washington, D.C.

Smith, Captain John, *A Sea Grammar*, 1627, London

Steel, David, *Elements and Practice of Rigging and Seamanship*, 1794

Stirling N.B., *Treasure Under the Sea*, 1957, Garden City, NY

Internet sites

http://www.blurtit.com/q208062.html

http://domeofthesky.com/clicks/oct.html

http://www.hasi.gr/instruments/ast35

http://www.jrank.org/history/pages/6287/Mediterranean-Trade.html#ixzz0wnCWMS2K

http://www.go-star.com/antiquing/poisonbottles.htm

http://www.sha.org/bottle/medicinal.htm

http://www.airwreck.com/bottles/bottles.html

http://home.vicnet.net.au/~pwguild/a-botls.htm

http://users.xplornet.com/%7Eshipping/Lloyds.htm

http://www.pro.rcip-chin.gc.ca/bd-dl/nav-ship-eng.jsp?emu=en.vessel:/Proxapp/ws/vessel/public

http://www.1902encyclopedia.com/A/ANC/anchor.htm

UNDERWATER ARCHAEOLOGY

We found these worksheets to be very valuable in recording information for cannon and anchors in order to help determine their age and origin.

Underwater Archaeological Anchor Data Sheet For Anchors With a Depleted Wooden Stock

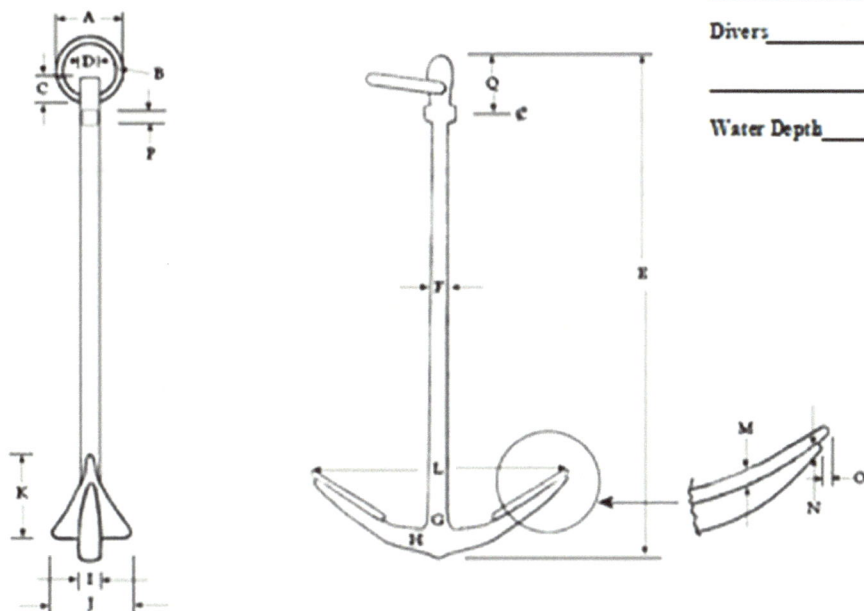

Artifact #_____

Artifact Date Estimate_____

Date_____

Site_____
_____

Divers_____
_____

Water Depth_____

GPS LOCATION OF ANCHOR____ _____ _____

METRIC ATTRIBUTES:

A. RING DIAMETER_____ _____ _____

B. RING THICKNESS_____ _____ _____ .

C. TOP OF SHANK TO BASE OF RING _____ .

D. TOP OF SHANK DIAMETER____ _____ _____

E. LENGTH OF SHANK_____ _____

F. MID-SHANK DIAMETER_____ _____ _____

G. BASAL SHANK DIAMETER___ _____ _____

H. ARM DIAMETER EACH SIDE OF SHANK

LEFT_____ .

RIGHT_____

I. THICKNESS OF ARM_____ _____ _____

J. WIDTH OF PALMS LEFT_____

RIGHT_____ _____

K. LENGTH OF PALMS LEFT_____

RIGHT_____ _____

L. DISTANCE BETWEEN ARM TIPS__ _____ .

M. PALM THICKNESS LEFT____ _____ _____

RIGHT_____ _____

N. ARM THICKNESS AT END OF PALM

LEFT_____ _____ _____

RIGHT_____ _____ _____

O. DISTANCE FROM END OF PALM TO END OF ARM____ _____ _____ _____

P. STOCK MOUNT DIMENSIONS _____
_____

Q. TOP OF SHANK TO CENTER OF STOCK

MOUNT____ _____ _____ _____

R. DIRECTION OF SHANK IN RELATION TO

NORTH____ _____ _____ _____
_____

S. ENCRUSTATION____ _____ _____ _____

T. VISIBLE MARKINGS ____ _____ _____
_____

Anchor Data Sheet

CANNON DATA SHEET

Site #_____   Divers:_____

Site Name_____

Date_____   Recorder:_____

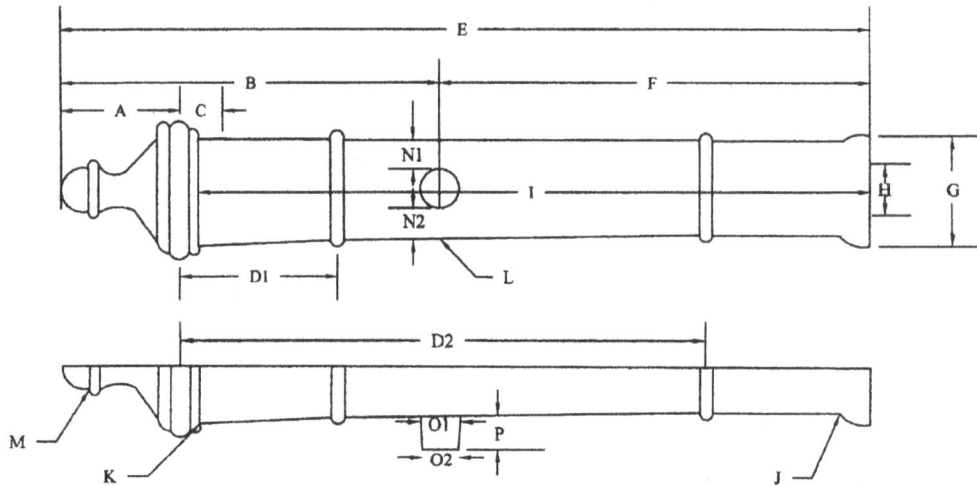

Site location and Reference:_____

DGPS Location of cannon :_____

Metric Attributes:
  Measurements requiring two readings for left and right sides should be taken viewing the cannon on the touch hole side from the cascabel down the tube.

A. Cascabel to breech reinforce_____

B. Cascabel to Trunion_____

C. Reinforce to Touch hole_____

D. Breech reinforce to each other reinforce band

	Distance	Thickness
1.	_____	_____
2.	_____	_____
3.	_____	_____
4.	_____	_____
5.	_____	_____
6.	_____	_____

E. Overall length_____

F. Trunion to muzzle length_____

G. Muzzle diameter_____

H. Bore diameter_____

I. Bore depth_____

J. Diameter behind muzzle flare_____

K. Diameter in front of breech reinforce_____

L. Diameter of tube at trunions_____

M. Diameter of cascabel_____

N. Vertical position of trunion on tube

  1. Trunion to dorsal_____

  2. Trunion to ventral_____

O. Diameter of trunion

  1. At tube   Left_____
               Right_____

  2. At ends   Left_____
               Right_____

P. Length of trunions

            Left_____

            Right_____

Non-Metric Attributes: Answer on reverse side

  1. Depth to and description of bottom.
  2. Type of sediment(s).
  3. Lifting handles: description & necessary accompanying measurements.
  4. Any other pertinent attributes: Distinguishing marks, insignias, dates, color, condition, type of metal, etc..
  5. Direction of cannon muzzel in relation to NORTH

Cannon Data Sheet

GLOSSARY OF NAUTICAL TERMS

From Wikipedia, the free encyclopedia

This is a **glossary of nautical terms**; some remain current, many date from the 17th 19th century.

A

- **Above board** – On or above the deck, in plain view, not hiding anything.
- **Above-water hull** – The hull section of a vessel above waterline, the visible part of a ship. Also, topsides.
- **Act of Pardon**, **Act of Grace** – A letter from a state or power authorizing action by a privateer. Also see Letter of marque.
- **Abaft** – Toward the stern, relative to some object ("abaft the fore hatch").
- **Abaft the beam** – Further aft than the beam: a relative bearing of greater than 90 degrees from the bow: "two points abaft the port beam".
- **Abandon ship!** – An imperative to leave the vessel immediately, usually in the face of some imminent danger.
- **Abeam** – *On the beam*, a relative bearing at right angles to the centerline of the ship's keel.
- **Abel Brown** – A sea song (shanty) about a young sailor trying to sleep with a maiden.[1]
- **Aboard** – On or in a vessel (see also "close aboard").
- **Absentee pennant** – Special pennant flown to indicate absence of commanding officer, admiral, his chief of staff, or officer whose flag is flying (division, squadron, or flotilla commander).
- **Absolute bearing** – The bearing of an object in relation to north. Either *true bearing*, using the geographical or true north, or *magnetic bearing*, using magnetic north. See also "bearing" and "relative bearing".
- **Accommodation ladder** – A portable flight of steps down a ship's side.
- **Admiral** – Senior naval officer of Flag rank. In ascending order of seniority, Rear Admiral, Vice Admiral, Admiral and Admiral of the Fleet (Royal Navy). Derivation Arabic, from *Amir al-Bahr* ("Ruler of the sea").
- **Admiralty** – A high naval authority in charge of a state's Navy or a major territorial component. In the Royal Navy (UK) the Board of Admiralty, executing the office of the Lord High Admiral, promulgates Naval law in the form of Queen's (or King's) Regulations and Admiralty Instructions.

- **Admiralty law** – Body of law that deals with maritime cases. In the UK administered by the Probate, Divorce and Admiralty Division of the High Court of Justice or supreme court.
- **Adrift** – Afloat and unattached in any way to the shore or seabed, but not under way. It implies that a vessel is not under control and therefore goes where the wind and current take her (*loose from moorings*, or *out of place*). Also refers to any gear not fastened down or put away properly. It can also be used to mean "absent without leave".
- **Advance note** – A note for one month's wages issued to sailors on their signing a ship's articles.
- **Aft** – Towards the stern (of the vessel).
- **Afloat** – Of a vessel which is floating freely (not aground or sunk). More generally of vessels in service ("the company has 10 ships afloat").
- **Afternoon watch** – The 1200-1600 watch.
- **Aground** – Resting on or touching the ground or bottom (usually involuntarily).
- **Ahead** – Forward of the bow.
- **Ahoy** – A cry to draw attention. Term used to hail a boat or a ship, as "*Boat ahoy!*"
- **Ahull** –
  1. When the boat is lying broadside to the sea.
  2. To ride out a storm with no sails and helm held to leeward.
- **Aid to Navigation** – (ATON) Any device external to a vessel or aircraft specifically intended to assist navigators in determining their position or safe course, or to warn them of dangers or obstructions to navigation.
- **All hands** – Entire ship's company, both officers and enlisted personnel.
- **All night in** – Having no night watches.
- **Aloft** – In the rigging of a sailing ship. Above the ship's uppermost solid structure; overhead or high above.
- **Alongside** – By the side of a ship or pier.
- **Amidships (or midships)** – In the middle portion of ship, along the line of the keel.
- **Anchor** – An object designed to prevent or slow the drift of a ship, attached to the ship by a line or chain; typically a metal, hook-like or plough-like object designed to grip the bottom under the body of water (but also see *sea anchor*).
- **Anchorage** – A suitable place for a ship to anchor. Area of a port or harbor.
- **Anchor's aweigh** – Said of an anchor when just clear of the bottom.
- **Anchor ball** – Round black shape hoisted in the forepart of a vessel to show that it is anchored.
- **Anchor buoy** – A small buoy secured by a light line to anchor to indicate position of anchor on bottom.

- **Anchor chain** or **anchor cable** – Chain connecting the ship to the anchor.
- **Anchor detail** – Group of men who handle ground tackle when the ship is anchoring or getting underway.
- **Anchor home** – The term for when the anchor is secured for sea. Typically rests just outside the hawse pipe on the outer side of the hull, at the bow of a vessel.
- **Anchor light** – White light displayed by a ship at anchor. Two such lights are displayed by a ship over 150 feet (46 m) in length.
- **Anchor rode** – The anchor line, rope or cable connecting the anchor chain to the vessel. Also Rode.
- **Anchor watch** – The crewmen assigned to take care of the ship while anchored or moored, charged with such duties as making sure that the anchor is holding and the vessel is not drifting. Most marine GPS units have an Anchor Watch alarm capability.
- **Andrew** – Traditional lower-deck slang term for the Royal Navy.
- **Anti-rolling tanks** — A pair of fluid-filled, usually water, tanks mounted on opposite sides of a ship below the waterline. Fluid would be pumped between them in an attempt to dampen the amount of roll.
- **Apparent wind** – The combination of the true wind and the headwind caused by the boat's forward motion. For example, it causes a light side wind to appear to come from well ahead of the beam.
- **Arc of Visibility** – The portion of the horizon over which a lighted aid to navigation is visible from seaward.
- **Armament** – A ship's weapons.
- **Articles of War** – Regulations governing the military and naval forces of UK and USA; read to every ship's company on commissioning and at specified intervals during the commission.
- **ASDIC** – A type of sonar used by the Allies for detecting submarines during the Second World War.
- **Ashore** – On the beach, shore or land.
- **Astern** – towards the stern (rear) of a vessel, behind a vessel.
- **Asylum Harbour** – A harbour used to provide shelter from a storm.
- **ASW** – Anti-submarine warfare.
- **Athwart, athwartships** – At right angles to the fore and aft or centerline of a ship
- **Avast** – Stop! Cease or desist from whatever is being done.
- **Awash** – So low in the water that the water is constantly washing across the surface.
- **Aweigh** – Position of an anchor just clear of the bottom.
- **Aye, aye** -- Reply to an order or command to indicate that it, firstly, is heard; and, secondly, is understood and will be carried out. ("Aye, aye, sir" to officers).
- **Azimuth compass** – An instrument employed for ascertaining position of the sun with respect to magnetic north. The azimuth of an

object is its bearing from the observer measured as an angle clockwise from true north.

- **Azimuth circle** – Instrument used to take bearings of celestial objects.

B

- **Back and fill** – To use the advantage of the tide being with you when the wind is not.
- **Backstays** – Long lines or cables, reaching from the stern of the vessel to the mast heads, used to support the mast.
- **Baggywrinkle** – A soft covering for cables (or any other obstructions) that prevents sail chafing from occurring.
- **Bailer** – A device for removing water that has entered the boat.
- **Bank** – A large area of elevated sea floor.
- **Banyan** – Traditional Royal Navy term for a day or shorter period of rest and relaxation.
- **Bar** – Large mass of sand or earth, formed by the surge of the sea. They are mostly found at the entrances of great rivers or havens, and often render navigation extremely dangerous, but confer tranquility once inside. See also: Touch and go, grounding. Alfred Lord Tennyson's poem "Crossing the bar", an allegory for death.
- **Bar pilot** – A bar pilot guides ships over the dangerous sandbars at the mouth of rivers and bays.
- **Barrelman** – A sailor that was stationed in the crow's nest.
- **Batten down the hatches** – To prepare for inclement weather.
- **Beaching** – Deliberately running a vessel *aground*, to load and unload (as with landing craft), or sometimes to prevent a damaged vessel sinking.
- **Beacon** – A lighted or unlighted fixed aid to navigation attached directly to the earth's surface. (Lights and daybeacons both constitute beacons.)
- **Beam** – The width of a vessel at the widest point, or a point alongside the ship at the mid-point of its length.
- **Beam ends** – The sides of a ship. "On her beam ends" may mean the vessel is literally on her side and possibly about to capsize; more often, the phrase means the vessel is listing 45 degrees or more.
- **Bear** – Large squared off stone used for scraping clean the deck of a sailing man-of-war.
- **Bear down** or **bear away** – Turn away from the wind, often with reference to a transit.
- **Bearing** – The horizontal direction of a line of sight between two objects on the surface of the earth. See also "absolute bearing" and "relative bearing".
- **Beating** – Sailing closer to the wind than about 60° (see also *reaching*, *running* and *tacking*).
- **Beaufort scale** – The scale describing wind force devised by Admiral Sir Francis Beaufort in 1808, in which winds are graded by the effect

of their force (originally, the amount of sail that a fully-rigged frigate could carry). Scale now reads up to Force 17.

- **Before the mast** – Literally, the area of a ship before the foremast (the forecastle). Most often used to describe men whose living quarters are located here, officers being quartered in the stern-most areas of the ship (near the quarterdeck). Officer-trainees lived between the two ends of the ship and become known as "midshipmen". Crew members who started out as seamen, then became midshipmen, and later, officers, were said to have gone from "one end of the ship to the other" (also see *hawsepiper*).
- **Belay** –
  1. To make fast a line around a fitting, usually a cleat or belaying pin.
  2. An order to halt a current activity or countermand an order prior to execution.
- **Belaying pins** – Bars of iron or hard wood to which running rigging may be secured, or *belayed*.
- **Bend** – A knot used to join two ropes or lines. Also see *hitch*.
- **Bermudan rig** – A triangular mainsail, without an upper spar, which is hoisted up the mast by a single halyard attached to the head of the sail. This configuration, introduced to Europe about 1920, allows the use of a tall mast, enabling sails to be set higher where wind speed is greater.
- **Berth (moorings)** – A location in a port or harbour used specifically for mooring vessels while not at sea.
- **Berth (sleeping)** – A bed or sleeping accommodation on a boat or ship.
- **Best bower (anchor)** – The larger of two anchors carried in the bow; so named as it was the last, *best* hope.
- **Between the devil and the deep blue sea** – See *devil seam*.
- **Bight** –
  1. Bight, a loop in rope or line – a hitch or knot tied *on the bight* is one tied in the middle of a rope, without access to the ends.
  2. An indentation in a coastline.
- **Bilge** – The bilge is the compartment at the bottom of the hull of a ship or boat where water collects so that it may be pumped out of the vessel at a later time.
- **Bilge keels** – A pair of keels on either side of the hull, usually slanted outwards. In yachts, they allow the use of a drying mooring, the boat standing upright on the keels (and often a *skeg*) when the tide is out.
- **Bilged on her anchor** – A ship that has run upon her own anchor, so the anchor cable runs under the hull.
- **Bimini top** – Open-front canvas top for the cockpit of a boat, usually supported by a metal frame.
- **Bimmy** – A punitive instrument
- **Binnacle** – The stand on which the ship's compass is mounted.

- **Binnacle list** – A ship's sick list. The list of men unable to report for duty was given to the officer or mate of the watch by the ship's surgeon. The list was kept at the binnacle.
- **Bitt** – A post mounted on the ship's bow, for fastening ropes or cables.
- **Bitter end** – The anchor cable is tied to the bitts, when the cable is fully paid out, the bitter end has been reached. The last part of a rope or cable.
- **Block** – A pulley or set of pulleys.
- **Blue Peter** – A blue and white flag (the flag for the letter "P") hoisted at the foretrucks of ships about to sail. Formerly a white ship on a blue ground, but later a white square on a blue ground.
- **Boat** – A craft or vessel designed to float on, and provide transport over, water.
- **Boat-hook** – A pole with a hook on the end, used to reach into the water to catch buoys or other floating objects.
- **Boatswain** or **bosun** (both pronounced /ˈboʊsən/) – A non-commissioned officer responsible for the sails, ropes and boats on a ship who issues "piped" commands to seamen.
- **Bobstay** – A stay which holds the bowsprit downwards, counteracting the effect of the forestay. Usually made of wire or chain to eliminate stretch.
- **Bollard** – From 'bol' or 'bole', the round trunk of a tree. A substantial vertical pillar to which lines may be made fast. Generally on the quayside rather than the ship.
- **Body plan** – In shipbuilding, an end elevation showing the contour of the sides of a ship at certain points of her length.
- **Bombay runner** – Large cockroach.
- **Bonded jacky** – A type of tobacco or sweet cake.
- **Booby** – A type of bird that has little fear and therefore is particularly easy to catch.
- **Booby hatch** – A sliding hatch or cover.
- **Boom** – A spar attached to the foot of a fore-and-aft sail.
- **Boom gallows** – A raised crossmember that supports a boom when the sail is lowered (obviates the need for a topping lift) .
- **Booms** – Masts or yards, lying on board in reserve.
- **Boom vang** or **vang** – A sail control that lets one apply downward tension on a boom, countering the upward tension provided by the sail. The boom vang adds an element of control to sail shape when the sheet is let out enough that it no longer pulls the boom down. Boom vang tension helps control leech twist, a primary component of sail power.
- **Bottlescrew** – A device for adjusting tension in stays, shrouds and similar lines.
- **Bottomry** – Pledging a ship as security in a financial transaction.
- **Bow** – The front of a ship.
- **Bow chaser** – See *chase gun*

- **Bowline** – A type of knot, producing a strong loop of a fixed size, topologically similar to a sheet bend. Also a rope attached to the side of a sail to pull it towards the bow (for keeping the windward edge of the sail steady).
- **Bowse** – To pull or hoist.
- **Bowsprit** – A spar projecting from the bow used as an anchor for the forestay and other rigging.
- **Bow thruster** – A small propeller or water-jet at the bow, used for manoeuvring larger vessels at slow speed. May be mounted externally, or in a tunnel running through the bow from side to side.
- **Boxing the compass** – To state all 36 points of the compass, starting at north, proceeding clockwise. Sometimes applied to a wind that is constantly shifting.
- **Boy Seaman** – a young sailor, still in training
- **Brail** – To furl or truss a sail by pulling it in towards the mast, or the ropes used to do so.
- **Brake** – The handle of the pump, by which it is worked.
- **Brass monkey** or **brass monkey weather** – Used in the expression "it is cold enough to freeze the balls off a brass monkey" (origin uncertain, see WP entry linked above)
- **Breakwater** — A structure built on the forecastle of a ship intended to divert water away from the forward superstructure or gun mounts.
- **Bridge** – A structure above the weather deck, extending the full width of the vessel, which houses a command centre, itself called by association, the bridge.
- **Bring to** – Cause a ship to be stationary by arranging the sails.
- **Broach** – When a sailing vessel loses control of its motion and is forced into a sudden sharp turn, often heeling heavily and in smaller vessels sometimes leading to a capsize. The change in direction is called *broaching-to*. Occurs when too much sail is set for a strong gust of wind, or in circumstances where the sails are unstable.
- **Buffer** – The chief bosun's mate (in the Royal Navy), responsible for discipline.
- **Bulkhead** – An upright wall within the hull of a ship. Particularly a watertight, load-bearing wall.
- **Bull of Barney** – A beast mentioned in an obscene sea proverb.
- **Bulwark** – The extension of the ship's side above the level of the weather deck.
- **Bumboat** – A private boat selling goods.
- **Bumpkin** or **boomkin** –
  1. A spar, similar to a bowsprit, but which projects from the stern. May be used to attach the backstay or mizzen sheets.
  2. An iron bar (projecting out-board from a ship's side) to which the lower and topsail brace blocks are sometimes hooked.
- **Bunting tosser** – A signalman who prepares and flies flag hoists. Also known in the American Navy as a skivvy waver.

- **Buntline** – One of the lines tied to the bottom of a square sail and used to haul it up to the yard when furling.
- **Buoy** – A floating object of defined shape and color, which is anchored at a given position and serves as an aid to navigation.
- **Buoyed up** – Lifted by a buoy, especially a cable that has been lifted to prevent it from trailing on the bottom.
- **Burgee** - A small flag, typically triangular, flown from the masthead of a yacht to indicate yacht-club membership.
- **By and large** – *By* means into the wind, while *large* means with the wind. "By and large" is used to indicate all possible situations "*the ship handles well both by and large*".
- **By the board** – Anything that has gone overboard.

C

- **Cabin** – an enclosed room on a deck or flat.
- **Cabin boy** – attendant on passengers and crew.
- **Cable** – A large rope.
- **Cable length** – A measure of length or distance. Equivalent to (UK) 1/10 nautical mile, approx. 600 feet; (USA) 120 fathoms, 720 feet (219 m); other countries use different values.
- **Canister** – a type of antipersonnel cannon load in which lead balls or other loose metallic items were enclosed in a tin or iron shell. On firing, the shell would disintegrate, releasing the smaller metal objects with a shotgun-like effect.
- **Canoe stern** – A design for the stern of a yacht which is pointed, like a bow, rather than squared off as a transom.
- **Cape Horn fever** – The name of the fake illness a malingerer is pretending to suffer from.
- **Capsize** – When a ship or boat lists too far and rolls over, exposing the keel. On large vessels, this often results in the sinking of the ship.
- **Capstan** – A large winch with a vertical axis. A full-sized human-powered capstan is a waist-high cylindrical machine, operated by a number of hands who each insert a horizontal *capstan bar* in holes in the capstan and walk in a circle. Used to wind in anchors or other heavy objects; and sometimes to administer flogging over.
- **Captain's daughter** – The cat o' nine tails, which in principle is only used on board on the captain's (or a court martial's) personal orders.
- **Cardinal** – Referring to the four main points of the compass: north, south, east and west. See also "bearing".
- **Careening** – Tilting a ship on its side, usually when beached, to clean or repair the hull below the water line.
- **Carvel built** - A method of constructing wooden hulls by fixing planks to a frame so that the planks butt up against each other. Cf "clinker built".
- **Cat** –
1. To prepare an anchor, after raising it by lifting it with a tackle to the *cat head*, prior to securing (*fishing*) it alongside for sea. (An anchor

raised to the cat head is said to be *catted*.)

2. The cat o' nine tails (see below).

3. A cat-rigged boat or *catboat*.

- **Catamaran** – A vessel with two hulls.
- **Catboat** – A cat-rigged vessel with a single mast mounted close to the bow, and only one sail, usually on a gaff.
- **Cat o' nine tails** – A short nine-tailed whip kept by the bosun's mate to flog sailors (and soldiers in the Army). When not in use, the cat was kept in a baize bag, hence the term "cat out of the bag". "Not enough room to swing a cat" also derives from this.
- **Cat head** – A beam extending out from the hull used to support an anchor when raised in order to secure or 'fish' it.
- **Centreboard** – A board or plate lowered through the hull of a dinghy on the centreline to resist leeway.
- **Chafing** – Wear on line or sail caused by constant rubbing against another surface.
- **Chafing gear** – Material applied to a line or spar to prevent or reduce chafing. See Baggywrinkle.
- **Chain-shot** – Cannon balls linked with chain used to damage rigging and masts.
- **Chain locker** – A space in the forward part of the ship, typically beneath the bow in front of the foremost collision bulkhead, that contains the anchor chain when the anchor is secured for sea.
- **Chain-wale or channel** – A broad, thick plank that projects horizontally from each of a ship's sides abreast a mast, distinguished as the fore, main, or mizzen channel accordingly, serving to extend the base for the shrouds, which supports the mast.
- **Chase gun**, **chase piece** or **chaser** – A cannon pointing forward or aft, often of longer range than other guns. Those on the bow (*bow chaser*) were used to fire upon a ship ahead, while those on the rear (*stern chaser*) were used to ward off pursuing vessels. Unlike guns pointing to the side, chasers could be brought to bear in a chase without slowing.
- **Cheeks** –

1. Wooden blocks at the side of a spar.

2. The sides of a block or gun-carriage.

- **Chine** –

1. A relatively sharp angle in the hull, as compared to the rounded bottoms of most traditional boat hulls.

2. A line formed where the sides of a boat meet the bottom. Soft chine is when the two sides join at a shallow angle, and hard chine is when they join at a steep angle.

- **Chock** – Hole or ring attached to the hull to guide a line via that point
- **Chock-a-block** – Rigging blocks that are so tight against one another that they cannot be further tightened.
- **Chronometer** - a timekeeper accurate enough to be used to determine longitude by means of celestial navigation.

- **Civil Red Ensign** – The British Naval Ensign or Flag of the *British Merchant Navy*, a red flag with the Union Flag in the upper left corner. Colloquially called the "red duster".
- **Clean bill of health** – A certificate issued by a port indicating that the ship carries no infectious diseases. Also called a pratique.
- **Clean slate** – At the helm, the watch keeper would record details of speed, distances, headings, etc. on a slate. At the beginning of a new watch the slate would be wiped clean.
- **Cleat** – A stationary device used to secure a rope aboard a vessel.
- **Clench** – A method of fixing together two pieces of wood, usually overlapping planks, by driving a nail through both planks as well as a washer-like rove. The nail is then burred or riveted over to complete the fastening.
- **Clew** – The lower corners of square sails or the corner of a triangular sail at the end of the boom.
- **Clew-lines** – Used to truss up the clews, the lower corners of square sails.
- **Clinker built** - A method of constructing hulls that involves overlapping planks, and/or plates, much like Viking longships, resulting in speed and flexibility in small boat hulls. Cf "carvel built".
- **Close aboard** – Near a ship.
- **Close-hauled** – Of a vessel *beating* as close to the wind direction as possible.
- **Club hauling** The ship drops one of its anchors at high speed to turn abruptly. This was sometimes used as a means to get a good firing angle on a pursuing vessel.
- **Coaming** – The raised edge of a hatch, cockpit or skylight to help keep out water.
- **Companionway** – A raised and windowed hatchway in the ship's deck, with a ladder leading below and the hooded entrance-hatch to the main cabins.
- **Communication tube** – A tube, usually armored, connecting the conning tower with the below-decks control spaces in warships.
- **Compass** – Navigational instrument showing the direction of the vessel in relation to the Earth's geographical poles or magnetic poles. Commonly consists of a magnet aligned with the Earth's magnetic field, but other technologies have also been developed, such as the gyrocompass.
- **Consort** – Unpowered Great Lakes vessels, usually a fully loaded schooner, barge, or steamer barge, towed by a larger steamer that would often tow more than one barge. The consort system was used in the Great Lakes from the 1860s to around 1920.
- **Corrector** – A device to correct the ship's compass, for example counteracting errors due to the magnetic effects of a steel hull.
- **Counter** – The part of the stern above the waterline that extends beyond the rudder stock culminating in a small transom. A long

counter increases the waterline length when the boat is heeled, so increasing hull speed.

- **Counterflood** – To deliberately flood compartments on the opposite side from already flooded ones. Usually done to reduce a list.
- **Courses** the lowest square sail on each mast– The mainsail, foresail, and the mizzen on a four masted ship (the after most mast usually sets a gaff driver or spanker instead of a square sail).
- **Coxswain** or **cockswain** – The helmsman or crew member in command of a boat.
- **As the crow flies** – A direct line between two points (which might cross land) which is the way crows travel rather than ships which must go around land.
- **Crance/Crans/Cranze iron** – A fitting, mounted at the end of a bowsprit to which stays are attached.
- **Cringle** – A rope loop, usually at the corners of a sail, for fixing the sail to a spar. They are often reinforced with a metal eye.
- **Cro'jack** or **crossjack** – a square yard used to spread the foot of a topsail where no course is set, e.g. on the foremast of a topsail schooner or above the driver on the mizzen mast of a ship rigged vessel.
- **Crow's nest** – Specifically a masthead constructed with sides and sometimes a roof to shelter the lookouts from the weather, generally by whaling vessels, this term has become a generic term for what is properly called masthead. See masthead.
- **Cross Trees** – A strong cross piece that allows to spread the top mast stays allowing for taller masts, larger top sails. Allows to extend the height of the ships mast.
- **Crutches** – Metal Y shaped pins to hold oars whilst rowing.
- **Cuddy** – A small cabin in a boat.
- **Cunningham** – A line invented by Briggs Cunningham, used to control the shape of a sail.
- **Cunt splice** or **cut splice** – A join between two lines, similar to an eye-splice, where each rope end is joined to the other a short distance along, making an opening which closes under tension.
- **Cuntline** – The "valley" between the strands of a rope or cable. Before serving a section of laid rope e.g. to protect it from chafing, it may be "wormed" by laying yarns in the cuntlines, giving that section an even cylindrical shape.
- **Cut and run** – When wanting to make a quick escape, a ship might cut lashings to sails or cables for anchors, causing damage to the rigging, or losing an anchor, but shortening the time needed to make ready by bypassing the proper procedures.
- **Cut of his jib** – The "cut" of a sail refers to its shape. Since this would vary between ships, it could be used both to identify a familiar vessel at a distance, and to judge the possible sailing qualities of an unknown one. Also used figuratively of people.

D

- **Daggerboard** – A type of light centerboard that is lifted vertically; often in pairs, with the leeward one lowered when beating.
- **Davy Jones' Locker** – An idiom for the bottom of the sea.
- **Day-blink** - Moment at dawn where, from some point on the mast, a lookout can see above low lying mist which envelops the ship.
- **Day beacon** – An unlighted fixed structure which is equipped with a dayboard for daytime identification.
- **Dayboard** – The daytime identifier of an aid to navigation presenting one of several standard shapes (square, triangle, rectangle) and colors (red, green, white, orange, yellow, or black).
- **Deadeye** – A wooden block with holes (but no pulleys) which is spliced to a shroud. It is used to adjust the tension in the standing rigging of large sailing vessels, by lacing through the holes with a lanyard to the deck. Performs the same job as a turnbuckle.
- **Deadrise** – The design angle between the keel (q.v.) and horizontal.
- **Dead run** – See *running*.
- **Deadwood** – A wooden part of the centerline structure of a boat, usually between the sternpost and amidships.
- **Decks** – the structures forming the approximately horizontal surfaces in the ship's general structure. Unlike flats, they are a structural part of the ship.
- **Deck hand**, **decky** – A person whose job involves aiding the deck supervisor in (un)mooring, anchoring, maintenance, and general evolutions on deck.
- **Deck supervisor** – The person in charge of all evolutions and maintenance on deck; sometimes split into two groups: forward deck supervisor, aft deck supervisor.
- **Deckhead** – The under-side of the deck above. Sometimes paneled over to hide the pipe work. This paneling, like that lining the bottom and sides of the holds, is the ceiling.
- **Derrick** – A lifting device composed of one mast or pole and a boom or jib which is hinged freely at the bottom.
- **Devil seam** – The devil was possibly a slang term for the garboard seam, hence "between the devil and the deep blue sea" being an allusion to keel hauling, but a more popular version seems to be the seam between the waterway and the stanchions which would be difficult to get at, requiring a cranked caulking iron, and a restricted swing of the caulking mallet.
- **Devil to pay** (or **devil to pay, and no pitch hot**) – 'Paying' the devil is sealing the *devil seam*. It is a difficult and unpleasant job (with no resources) because of the shape of the seam (up against the stanchions) or if the devil refers to the garboard seam, it must be done with the ship slipped or careened.
- **Directional light** – A light illuminating a sector or very narrow angle and intended to mark a direction to be followed.

- **Displacement** – The weight of water displaced by the immersed volume of a ship's hull, exactly equivalent to the weight of the whole ship.
- **Displacement hull** – A hull designed to travel through the water, rather than planing over it.
- **Disrate** – To reduce in rank or rating; demote.
- **Dodger** - a hood forward of a hatch or cockpit to protect the crew from wind and spray. Can be soft or hard.
- **Dog watch** – A short watch period, generally half the usual time (e.g. a two hour watch between two four hour ones). Such a watch might be included in order to slowly rotate the system over several days for fairness, or to allow both watches to eat their meals at approximately normal times.
- The **Doldrums** – Also called the "equatorial calms", is a nautical term for the equatorial trough, with special reference to the light and variable nature of the winds.[2]
- **Dolphin** – A structure consisting of a number of piles driven into the seabed or riverbed in a circular pattern and drawn together with wire rope.
- **Downhaul** – A line used to control either a mobile spar, or the shape of a sail. A downhaul can also be used to retrieve a sail back on deck.
- **Draft** or **draught** (both pronounced /ˈdrɑːft/) – The depth of a ship's keel below the waterline.
- **Dressing down**
  1 – Treating old sails with oil or wax to renew them.
  2 – A verbal reprimand.
- **Driver** – The large sail flown from the mizzen gaff.
- **Driver-mast** – The fifth mast of a six-masted barquentine or gaff schooner. It is preceded by the jigger mast and followed by the spanker mast. The sixth mast of the only seven-masted vessel, the gaff schooner *Thomas W. Lawson*, was normally called the pusher-mast.
- **Dunnage** –
  1. Loose packing material used to protect a ship's cargo from damage during transport.
  2. Personal baggage.

E

- **Earrings** – Small lines, by which the uppermost corners of the largest sails are secured to the yardarms.
- **Echo sounding** – Measuring the depth of the water using a sonar device. Also see *sounding* and *swinging the lead*.
- **Embayed** – The condition where a sailing vessel (especially one which sails poorly to windward) is confined between two capes or headlands by a wind blowing directly onshore.
- *En echelon* gun turrets - forward and aft turrets on opposite sides of the ship.

- **Engine order telegraph** – a communications device used by the pilot to order engineers in the engine room to power the vessel at a certain desired speed. Also **Chadburn**.
- **Extremis** – (also known as "in extremis") the point under International Rules of the Road (Navigation Rules) at which the privileged (or stand-on) vessel on collision course with a burdened (or give-way) vessel determines it must maneuver to avoid a collision. Prior to extremis, the privileged vessel must maintain course and speed and the burdened vessel must maneuver to avoid collision.

F

- **Fair** –
  1. A smooth curve, usually referring to a line of the hull which has no deviations.
  2. To make something flush.
  3. A rope is fair when it has a clear run.
  4. A wind or current is fair when it offers an advantage to a boat.
- **Fairlead** – A ring, hook or other device used to keep a line or chain running in the correct direction or to prevent it rubbing or fouling.
- **Fall off** – To change the direction of sail so as to point in a direction that is more down wind. To bring the bow leeward. Also bear away, bear off or head down. The opposite of heading up.
- **Fardage** – Wood placed in bottom of ship to keep cargo dry.
- **Fast** – Fastened or held firmly (*fast aground*: stuck on the seabed; *made fast*: tied securely).
- **Fathom** – A unit of length equal to 6 feet (1.8 m), roughly measured as the distance between a man's outstretched hands. Particularly used to measure depth.
- **Fender** – An air or foam filled bumper used in boating to keep boats from banging into docks or each other.
- **Fetch** –
  1. The distance across water which a wind or waves have traveled.
  2. To reach a mark without tacking.
- **Fid** –
  1. A tapered wooden tool used for separating the strands of rope for splicing.
  2. A bar used to fix an upper mast in place.
- **Figurehead** – symbolic image at the head of a traditional sailing ship or early steamer.
- **Fireroom** - The compartment in which the ship's boilers or furnaces are stoked and fired.
- **Fire ship** – A ship loaded with flammable materials and explosives and sailed into an enemy port or fleet either already burning or ready to be set alight by its crew (who would then abandon it) in order to collide with and set fire to enemy ships.

- **First-rate** – The classification for the largest sailing warships of the 17th through 19th centuries. They had 3 masts, 850+ crew and 100+ guns.
- **Fish** –
  1. To repair a mast or spar with a fillet of wood.
  2. To secure an anchor on the side of the ship for sea (otherwise known as "catting".)
- **First Lieutenant** – In the Royal Navy, the senior lieutenant on board; responsible to the Commander for the domestic affairs of the ship's company. Also known as 'Jimmy the One' or 'Number One'. Removes his cap when visiting the mess decks as token of respect for the privacy of the crew in those quarters. Officer i/c cables on the forecastle. In the U.S. Navy the senior person in charge of all Deck hands.
- **First Mate** – The Second in command of a ship.
- **Fixed propeller** – A propeller mounted on a rigid shaft protruding from the hull of a vessel, usually driven by an inboard motor; steering must be done using a rudder. See also *outboard motor* and *sterndrive*.
- **Flag hoist** – A number of signal flags strung together to convey a message, e.g. 'England expects'.
- **Flank** – The maximum speed of a ship. Faster than "full speed".
- **Flare** –
  1. A curvature of the topsides outward towards the gunwale.
  2. A pyrotechnic signalling device, usually used to indicate distress.
- **Flatback** – A Great Lakes slang term for a vessel without any self unloading equipment.
- **Flotsam** – Debris or cargo that remains afloat after a shipwreck. See also jetsam.
- **Fluke** – The wedge-shaped part of an anchor's arms that digs into the bottom.
- **Fly by night** – A large sail used only for sailing downwind, requiring little attention.
- **Folding propeller** – A propeller with folding blades, furling to reduce drag on a sailing vessel when not in use.
- **Following sea** – Wave or tidal movement going in the same direction as a ship
- **Foot** –
  1. The lower edge of any sail.
  2. The bottom of a mast.
  3. A measurement of 12 inches.
- **Footloose** – If the foot of a sail is not secured properly, it is footloose, blowing around in the wind.
- **Footrope** – Each yard on a square rigged sailing ship is equipped with a footrope for sailors to stand on while setting or stowing the sails
- **Force** – See *Beaufort scale*.

- **Fore**, **foreward** (often written "for'ard") – Towards the bow (of the vessel).
- **Forecastle** – A partial deck, above the upper deck and at the head of the vessel; traditionally the sailors' living quarters. Pronounced /ˈfoʊksəl/, "fo'csle". The name is derived from the castle fitted to bear archers in time of war.
- **Forefoot** – The lower part of the stem of a ship.
- **Foremast jack** – An enlisted sailor, one who is housed before the foremast.
- **Forestays** – Long lines or cables, reaching from the bow of the vessel to the mast heads, used to support the mast.
- **Foul** –
  1. The opposite of clear. For instance, a rope is foul when it does nor run straight or smoothly, and an anchor is foul when it is caught on an obstruction.
  2. A breach of racing rules.
- **Founder** – To fill with water and sink → *Founder (Wiktionary)*
- **Frame** – A transverse structural member which gives the hull strength and shape. Wooden frames may be sawn, bent or laminated into shape. Planking is then fastened to the frames. A bent frame is called a timber.
- **Freeboard** – The height of a ship's hull (excluding superstructure) above the waterline. The vertical distance from the current waterline to the lowest point on the highest continuous watertight deck. This usually varies from one part to another.
- **Full and by** – Sailing into the wind (*by*), but not as close-hauled as might be possible, so as to make sure the sails are kept *full*. This provides a margin for error to avoid being taken aback (a serious risk for square-rigged vessels) in a tricky sea. Figuratively it implies getting on with the job but in a steady, relaxed way, without undue urgency or strain.
- **Furl** – To roll or gather a sail against its mast or spar.
- **Futtocks** – Pieces of timber that make up a large transverse frame.

G

- **Gaff** –
  1. The spar that holds the upper edge of a four-sided fore-and-aft mounted sail.
  2. A hook on a long pole to haul fish in.
- **Gaff rigged** – A boat rigged with a four-sided fore-and-aft sail with its upper edge supported by a spar or *gaff* which extends aft from the mast.
- **Gaff vang** – A line rigged to the end of a gaff and used to adjust a gaff sail's trim.
- **Gam** – A meeting of two (or more) whaling ships at sea. The ships each send out a boat to the other, and the two captains meet on one ship, while the two chief mates meet on the other.[3]

- **Gammon iron** – The bow fitting which clamps the bowsprit to the stem.
- **Galley** – the kitchen of the ship
- **Gangplank** – A movable bridge used in boarding or leaving a ship at a pier; also known as a "brow".
- **Gangway** – An opening in the bulwark of the ship to allow passengers to board or leave the ship.
- **Garbling** – The (illegal) practice of mixing cargo with garbage.
- **Garboard** – The strake closest to the keel (from Dutch *gaarboard*).
- **Garboard planks** – The planks immediately either side of the keel.
- **Gennaker** - A large, lightweight sail used for sailing a fore-and-aft rig down or across the wind, intermediate between a genoa and a spinnaker.
- **Genoa** or **genny** (both pronounced /d͡ʒɛni/) – A large *jib*, strongly overlapping the mainmast.
- **Ghost** – To sail slowly when there is apparently no wind.
- **Gibe** – See **gybe**.
- **Give-way (vessel)** – Where two vessels are approaching one another so as to involve a risk of collision, this is the vessel which is directed to keep out of the way of the other.
- **Global Positioning System** – (GPS) A satellite based radionavigation system providing continuous worldwide coverage. It provides navigation, position, and timing information to air, marine, and land users.
- **Going about** or **tacking** – Changing from one tack to another by going through the wind (see also *gybe*). When ready to go about the helmsman or skipper calls "Ready about", the crew then each call "Ready!", and as the turn is made the helmsman calls "Lee oh!".
- **Gooseneck** – Fitting that attaches the boom to the mast, allowing it to move freely.
- **Goosewinged** – Of a fore-and-aft rigged vessel sailing directly away from the wind, with the sails set on opposite sides of the vessel – for example with the mainsail to port and the jib to starboard, to maximize the amount of canvas exposed to the wind. Also see *running*.
- **Grapeshot** – Small balls of lead fired from a cannon, analogous to shotgun shot but on a larger scale. Similar to canister shot but with larger individual shot. Used to injure personnel and damage rigging more than to cause structural damage.
- **Grave** – To clean a ship's bottom.
- **Grog** – Watered-down pusser's rum consisting of half a gill with equal part of water, issued to all seamen over twenty. (CPOs and POs were issued with neat rum) From the British Admiral Vernon who, in 1740, ordered the men's ration of rum to be watered down. He was called "Old Grogram" because he often wore a grogram coat), and the watered rum came to be called 'grog'. Often used (illegally) as currency in exchange for favors in quantities prescribed as 'sippers'

and 'gulpers'. Additional issues of grog were made on the command 'splice the mainbrace' for celebrations or as a reward for performing especially onerous duties. The RN discontinued the practice of issuing rum in 1970. A sailor might repay a colleague for a favour by giving him part or all of his grog ration, ranging from "sippers" (a small amount) via "gulpers" (a larger quantity) to "grounders" (the entire tot).

- **Groggy** – Drunk from having consumed a lot of grog.
- **Ground** – The bed of the sea.
- **Grounding** – When a ship (while afloat) touches the bed of the sea, or goes "aground" (*qv*).
- **Gunport** — The opening in the side of the ship or in a turret through which the gun fires or protrudes.
- **Gunner's daughter** – see *kissing the gunner's daughter*.
- **Gunwale** ("gun'll") – Upper edge of the hull.
- **Gybe** or **jibe** (both pronounced /dʒaɪb/) – To change from one tack to the other away from the wind, with the stern of the vessel turning through the wind. When ready to gybe the helmsman or skipper calls "Ready to gybe", the crew then each call "Ready!", and as the turn is made the helmsman calls "Gybe oh!". A gybe may also happen accidentally when sailing downwind. (See also *going about* and *wearing ship*.)

H

- **Half-breadth plan** – In shipbuilding, a elevation of the lines of a ship, viewed from above and divided lengthwise.
- **Halyard** or **halliard** – Originally, ropes used for hoisting a spar with a sail attached; today, a line used to raise the head of any sail.
- **Hammock** – Canvas sheets, slung from the deckhead in messdecks, in which seamen slept. "Lash up and stow" a piped command to tie up hammocks and stow them (typically) in racks inboard of the ship's side to protect crew from splinters from shot and provide a ready means of preventing flooding caused by damage.
- **Handy billy** – A loose block and tackle with a hook or tail on each end, which can be used wherever it is needed. Usually made up of one single and one double block.
- **Hand bomber** – A ship using coal-fired boilers shoveled in by hand.
- **Hand over fist** – To climb steadily upwards, from the motion of a sailor climbing shrouds on a sailing ship (originally "hand over hand").
- **Handsomely** – With a slow even motion, as when hauling on a line "handsomely".
- **Hank** – A fastener attached to the luff of the headsail that attaches the headsail to the forestay. Typical designs include a bronze or plastic hook with a spring-operated gate, or a strip of cloth webbing with a snap fastener.

- **Harbor** – A harbor or harbour, or haven, is a place where ships may shelter from the weather or are stored. Harbours can be man-made or natural.
- **Hard** – A section of otherwise muddy shoreline suitable for mooring or hauling out.
- **Harden up** – Turn towards the wind; sail closer to the wind.
- **Hardtack** – A hard and long-lasting dry biscuit, used as food on long journeys. Also called *ship's biscuit*.
- **Hatchway**, **hatch** – A covered opening in a ship's deck through which cargo can be loaded or access made to a lower deck; the cover to the opening is called a hatch.
- **Hauling wind** – Pointing the ship towards the direction of the wind; generally not the fastest point of travel on a sailing vessel.
- **Hawse pipe**, **hawse-hole** or **hawse** – The shaft or hole in the side of a vessel's bow through which the anchor chain passes.
- **Hawsepiper** – An informal term for a merchant ship's officer who began their career as an unlicensed merchant seaman, and so did not attend a traditional maritime academy to earn their officer's licence (also see *before the mast*).
- **Hawser** – Large rope used for mooring or towing a vessel.
- **Head** – The toilet or latrine of a vessel, which in sailing ships projected from the bows
- **Head of navigation** – A term used to describe the farthest point above the mouth of a river that can be navigated by ships.
- **Head sea** - A sea where waves are directly opposing the motion of the ship.
- **Headsail** – Any sail flown in front of the most forward mast.
- **Heave** – A vessel's transient, vertical, up-and-down motion.
- **Heaving to** – Stopping a sailing vessel by lashing the helm in opposition to the sails. The vessel will gradually drift to leeward, the speed of the drift depending on the vessel's design.
- **Heave down** – Turn a ship on its side (for cleaning).
- **Heeling** – Heeling is the lean caused by the wind's force on the sails of a sailing vessel.
- **Helmsman** – A person who steers a ship
- **Highfield lever** – A particular type of tensioning lever, usually for running backstays. Their use allows the leeward backstay to be completely slackened so that the boom can be let fully out.
- **Hitch** – A knot used to tie a rope or line to a fixed object. Also see *bend*.
- **Hog** –
  1. A fore-and-aft structural member of the hull fitted over the keel to provide a fixing for the garboard planks.
  2. A rough flat scrubbing brush for cleaning a ship's bottom under water.

- **Hogging** – When the peak of a wave is amidships, causing the hull to bend so the ends of the keel are lower than the middle. The opposite of *sagging*.
- **Hold** – In earlier use, below the orlop deck, the lower part of the interior of a ship's hull, especially when considered as storage space, as for cargo. In later merchant vessels it extended up through the decks to the underside of the weather deck.
- **Holiday** – A gap in the coverage of newly applied paint, slush, tar or other preservative.
- **Holystone** – A chunk of sandstone used to scrub the decks. The name comes from both the kneeling position sailors adopt to scrub the deck (reminiscent of genuflection for prayer), and the stone itself (which resembled a Bible in shape and size).
- **Horn** – A sound signal which uses electricity or compressed air to vibrate a disc diaphragm.
- **Horn timber** – A fore-and-aft structural member of the hull sloping up and backwards from the keel to support the counter.
- **Horse** –
  1. Attachment of sheets to deck of vessel (main-sheet horse).
  2. (v.) To move or adjust sail by brute hand force rather than using running rigging.
- **Hounds** – Attachments of stays to masts.
- **Hull** – The shell and framework of the basic flotation-oriented part of a ship.
- **Hull-down** – Of a vessel when only its upper parts are visible over the horizon.
- **Hull speed** – The maximum efficient speed of a displacement-hulled vessel.
- **Hydrofoil** – A boat with wing-like foils mounted on struts below the hull, lifting the hull entirely out of the water at speed and allowing water resistance to be greatly reduced.

I

- **Icing** – A serious hazard where cold temperatures (below about -10°C) combined with high wind speed (typically force 8 or above on the Beaufort scale) result in spray blown off the sea freezing immediately on contact with the ship
- **Idlers** – Members of a ship's company not required to serve watches. These were in general specialist tradesmen such as the carpenter and the sailmaker.
- **Inboard motor** – An engine mounted within the hull of a vessel, usually driving a fixed propeller by a shaft protruding through the stern. Generally used on larger vessels. Also see *sterndrive* and *outboard motor*.
- **Inboard-Outboard drive system** – See *sterndrive*.
- **Inglefield clip** – A type of clip for attaching a flag to a flag halyard.

- **In irons** – When the bow of a sailboat is headed into the wind and the boat has stalled and is unable to maneuver
- **In the offing** – In the water visible from on board a ship, now used to mean something imminent.
- **In-water survey** – a method of surveying the underwater parts of a ship while it is still afloat instead of having to drydock it for examination of these areas as was conventionally done.
- **Island** – The superstructure of an aircraft carrier. A carrier that lacks one is said to be flush decked.

J

- **Jack** –
  1 – A sailor. Also *jack tar* or just *tar*.
  2 – A flag. Typically the flag was talked about as if it were a member of the crew. Strictly speaking, a flag is only a "jack" if it is worn at the jackstaff at the bow of a ship.
- **Jacklines** or **jack stays** – Lines, often steel wire with a plastic jacket, from the bow to the stern on both port and starboard. The Jack Lines are used to clip on the safety harness to secure the crew to the vessel while giving them the freedom to walk on the deck.
- **Jack Tar** – A sailor dressed in 'square rig' with square collar. Formerly with a tarred pigtail.
- **Jenny** – See *genoa*
- **Jetsam** – Debris ejected from a ship that sinks or washes ashore. See also flotsam.
- **Jib** – A triangular staysail at the front of a ship.
- **Jibboom** – A spar used to extend the bowsprit.
- **Jibe** – See *gybe*.
- **Jigger-mast** – The fourth mast, although ships with four or more masts were uncommon, or the aft most mast where it is smallest on vessels of less than four masts.
- **Jollies** – Traditional Royal Navy nickname for the Royal Marines.
- **Joggle** – a slender triangular recess cut into the faying surface of a frame or steamed timber to fit over the land of clinker planking, or cut into the faying edge of a plank or rebate to avoid feather ends on a strake of planking. The feather end is cut off to produce a nib. The joggle and nib in this case is made wide enough to allow a caulking iron to enter the seam.
- **Junk** – Old cordage past its useful service life as lines aboard ship. The strands of old junk were teased apart in the process called picking oakum.
- **Jury rig** – Both the act of rigging a temporary mast and sails and the name of the resulting rig. A jury rig would be built at sea when the original rig was damaged, then it would be used to sail to a harbor or other safe place for permanent repairs.

K

- **Keel** – The central structural basis of the hull

- **Keelhauling** – Maritime punishment: to punish by dragging under the keel of a ship.
- **Kelson** – The timber immediately above the keel of a wooden ship.
- **Killick** – A small anchor. A fouled killick is the substantive badge of non-commissioned officers in the RN. Seamen promoted to the first step in the promotion ladder are called 'Killick'. The badge signifies that here is an Able Seaman skilled to cope with the awkward job of dealing with a fouled anchor.
- **Kissing the gunner's daughter** – bend over the barrel of a gun for punitive beating with a cane or cat
- **King plank** – The centerline plank of a laid deck. Its sides are often recessed, or nibbed, to take the ends of their parallel curved deck planks.
- **Kitchen rudder** – Hinged cowling around a fixed propeller, allowing the drive to be directed to the side or forwards to manoeuvre the vessel.
- **Knee** – Connects two parts roughly at right angles, e.g. deck beams to frames.
- **Knockdown** The condition of a sailboat being pushed abruptly to horizontal, with the mast parallel to the water surface.
- **Knot** – A unit of speed: 1 nautical mile (1.8520 km; 1.1508 mi) per hour. Originally speed was measured by paying out a line from the stern of a moving boat. The line had a knot every 47 feet 3 inches (14.40 m), and the number of knots passed out in 30 seconds gave the speed through the water in nautical miles per hour.
- **Know the ropes** – A sailor who 'knows the ropes' is familiar with the miles of cordage and ropes involved in running a ship.

L

- **Ladder** – On board a ship, all "stairs" are called ladders, except for literal staircases aboard passenger ships. Most "stairs" on a ship are narrow and nearly vertical, hence the name. Believed to be from the Anglo-Saxon word hiaeder, meaning ladder.
- **Laker** –Great Lakes slang for a vessel who spends all its time on the 5 Great Lakes.
- **Land lubber** – A person unfamiliar with being on the sea.
- **Lanyard** – A rope that ties something off.
- **Larboard** – Obsolete term for the left side of a ship. Derived from "lay-board" providing access between a ship and a quay, when ships normally docked with the left side to the wharf. Replaced by *port side* or *port*, to avoid confusion with *starboard*.
- **Large** – See **by and large**.
- **Lateral system** – A system of aids to navigation in which characteristics of buoys and beacons indicate the sides of the channel or route relative to a conventional direction of buoyage (usually upstream).

- **Lay** – To come and go, used in giving orders to the crew, such as "lay forward" or "lay aloft". To direct the course of vessel. Also, to twist the strands of a rope together.
- **Laying down** – Beginning construction in a shipyard.
- **Lazarette** – Small stowage locker at the aft end of a boat.
- **League** – A unit of length, normally equal to three nautical miles.
- **Leech** – The aft or trailing edge of a fore-and-aft sail; the leeward edge of a spinnaker; a vertical edge of a square sail. The leech is susceptible to twist, which is controlled by the boom vang, mainsheet and, if rigged with one, the gaff vang.
- **Lee side** – The side of a ship sheltered from the wind (cf. weather side).
- **Lee shore** – A shore downwind of a ship. A ship which cannot sail well to windward risks being blown onto a lee shore and grounded.
- **Leeboard** – A fin mounted on the side of a boat (usually in pairs) that can be lowered on the lee side of the ship to reduce leeway (similarly to a centerboard, which see).
- **Leeway** – The amount that a ship is blown leeward by the wind. See also *weatherly*.
- **Leeward** – In the direction that the wind is blowing towards.
- **Length overall, LOA** – the length of a ship.
- **Let go and haul** – An order indicating that the ship is now on the desired course relative to the wind and that the sails should be trimmed ('hauled') to suit.
- **Letter of marque and reprisal** – A warrant granted to a privateer condoning specific acts of piracy against a target as a redress for grievances.
- **Lifebelt**, **lifejacket**, **life preserver** or **Mae West** – A device such as a buoyant ring or inflatable jacket which keeps a person afloat in the water.
- **Lifeboat** –
  1. Shipboard lifeboat, kept on board a vessel and used to take crew and passengers to safety in the event of the ship being abandoned.
  2. Rescue lifeboat, usually launched from shore, used to rescue people from the water or from vessels in difficulty.
- **Liferaft** – An inflatable, covered raft, used in the event of a vessel being abandoned.
- **Line** – the correct nautical term for the majority of the cordage or "ropes" used on a vessel. A line will always have a more specific name, such as mizzen topsail halyard, which describes its use.
- **Line astern** – in naval warfare, a line of battle formed behind a flagship
- **Liner** – Ship of the line: a major warship capable of taking its place in the main (battle) line of fighting ships. Hence modern term for prestigious passenger vessels: ocean liner.

- **List** – The vessel's angle of lean or tilt to one side, in the direction called roll. Typically refers to a lean caused by flooding or improperly loaded or shifted cargo (as opposed to 'heeling', which see).
- **Loaded to the gunwales** – Literally, having cargo loaded as high as the ship's rail; also means extremely drunk.
- **Lofting** – The technique used to convert a scaled drawing to full size used in boat construction.
- **Loggerhead** – An iron ball attached to a long handle, used for driving caulking into seams and (occasionally) in a fight. Hence: 'at loggerheads'.
- **Long stay** – A description for the relative slackness of an anchor chain; this term means taught and extended.
- **Loose cannon** – An irresponsible and reckless individual whose behavior (either intended or unintended) endangers the group he or she belongs to. A loose cannon, weighing thousands of pounds, would crush anything and anyone in its path, and possibly even break a hole in the hull, thus endangering the seaworthiness of the whole ship.
- **Loose footed** – A mainsail that is not connected to a boom along its foot.
- **Lubber's hole** – A port cut into the bottom of the mizzentop (crow's-nest) allowing easy entry and exit. It was considered "un-seamanlike" to use this easier method rather than going over the side from the shrouds, and few sailors would risk the scorn of their shipmates by doing so (at least if there were witnesses)
- **Lubber's line** – A vertical line inside a compass case indicating the direction of the ship's head.
- **Luff** – The forward edge of a sail.
- **Luff up** – To steer a sailing vessel more towards the direction of the wind until the pressure is eased on the [sheet].
- **Luffing**
  1. When a sailing vessel is steered far enough to windward that the sail is no longer completely filled with wind (the luff of a fore-and-aft sail begins to flap first).
  2. Loosening a sheet so far past optimal trim that the sail is no longer completely filled with wind.
  3. The flapping of the sail(s) which results from having no wind in the sail at all.
- **Luff and touch her** - To bring the vessel so close to wind that the sails shake.[4]
- **Lying ahull** – Waiting out a storm by dousing all sails and simply letting the boat drift.
- **Lumber hooker** is a nautical term for a Great Lakes ship designed to carry her own deck load of lumber and to tow one or two barges. The barges were big old schooners stripped of their masts and running gear to carry large cargoes of lumber.
- **Lugger** - A ship rigged with lugsails.

- **Lugsail** - A four-sided fore-and-aft sail supported by a spar along the top that is fixed to the mast at a point some distance from the center of the spar. See Lugger.

M

- **Mae West** – A Second World War personal flotation device used to keep people afloat in the water; named after the 1930s actress Mae West, well-known for her large bosom.
- **Magnetic bearing** – An absolute bearing (*qv*) using magnetic north.
- **Magnetic north** – The direction towards the North Magnetic Pole. Varies slowly over time.
- **Mainbrace** – One of the braces attached to the mainmast.
- **Making way** – When a vessel is moving under its own power.
- **Mainmast** (or Main) – The tallest mast on a ship.
- **Mainsheet** – Sail control line that allows the most obvious effect on mainsail trim. Primarily used to control the angle of the boom, and thereby the mainsail, this control can also increase or decrease downward tension on the boom while sailing upwind, significantly affecting sail shape. For more control over downward tension on the boom, use a boom vang.
- **Man-of-war** or **man o' war** – a warship from the Age of Sail
- **Man overboard!** – A cry let out when a seaman has gone 'overboard' (fallen from the ship into the water).
- **Marconi rig** – Another term for Bermudan rig. The mainsail is triangular, rigged fore-and-aft with the lead edge fixed to the mast. Refers to the similarity of the tall mast to a radio aerial.
- **Marina** – a docking facility for small ships and yachts.
- **Marines** Soldiers afloat. Royal Marines formed as the Duke of York and Albany's Maritime Regiment of Foot in 1664 with many and varied duties including providing guard to ship's officers should there be mutiny aboard. Sometimes thought by seamen to be rather gullible, hence the phrase "tell it to the marines".
- **Marlinspike** – A tool used in ropework for tasks such as unlaying rope for splicing, untying knots, or forming a makeshift handle.
- **Mast** – A vertical pole on a ship which supports sails or rigging.
- **Masthead** – A small platform partway up the mast, just above the height of the mast's main yard. A lookout is stationed here, and men who are working on the main yard will embark from here. See also Crow's Nest.
- **Master** – Either the commander of commercial vessel, or a senior officer of a naval sailing ship in charge of routine seamanship and navigation but not in command during combat.
- **Master-at-arms** – A non-commissioned officer responsible for discipline on a naval ship. Standing between the officers and the crew, commonly known in the Royal Navy as 'the Buffer'.
- **Matelot** – A traditional Royal Navy term for an ordinary sailor.

- **Mess** – An eating place aboard ship. A group of crew who live and feed together,
- **Mess deck catering** – A system of catering in which a standard ration is issued to a mess supplemented by a money allowance which may be used by the mess to buy additional victuals from the pusser's stores or elsewhere. Each mess was autonomous and self-regulating. Seaman cooks, often members of the mess, prepared the meals and took them, in a tin canteen, to the galley to be cooked by the ship's cooks. As distinct from "cafeteria messing" where food is issued to the individual hand, which now the general practice.
- **Midshipman** – A non-commissioned officer below the rank of Lieutenant. Usually regarded as being "in training" to some degree. Also known as 'Snotty'. 'The lowest form of animal life in the Royal Navy' where he has authority over and responsibility for more junior ranks, yet, at the same time, relying on their experience and learning his trade from them.
- **Midshipman's nuts** – Broken pieces of biscuit as dessert.[5]
- **Midshipman's roll** – A slovenly method of rolling up a hammock transversely, and lashing it endways by one clue.[5]
- **Midshipman's hitch** – An alternative to the Blackwall hitch, preferred if the rope is greasy. Made by first forming a Blackwall hitch and then taking the underneath part and placing over the bill of the hook.[6]
- **Mile** – see *nautical mile*.
- **Mizzenmast** (or Mizzen) – The third mast, or mast aft of the mainmast, on a ship.
- **Mizzen staysail** – Sail on a ketch or yawl, usually lightweight, set from, and forward of, the mizzen mast while reaching in light to moderate air.
- **Monkey's fist** – a ball woven out of line used to provide heft to heave the line to another location. The monkey fist and other heaving-line knots were sometimes weighted with lead (easily available in the form of foil used to seal e.g. tea chests from dampness) although Clifford W. Ashley notes that there was a "definite sporting limit" to the weight thus added.
- **Moor** – to attach a boat to a mooring buoy or post. Also, to a dock a ship.
- **Mould** – A template of the shape of the hull in transverse section. Several moulds are used to form a temporary framework around which a hull is built.

N

- **Nautical mile** – A distance of 1.852 kilometres (1.151 mi). Approximately the distance of one minute of arc of latitude on the Earth's surface. A speed of one nautical mile per hour is called a *knot* (*qv*).

- **Navigation rules** – Rules of the road that provide guidance on how to avoid collision and also used to assign blame when a collision does occur.
- **Nipper** – Short rope used to bind a cable to the "messenger" (a moving line propelled by the capstan) so that the cable is dragged along too (used where the cable is too large to be wrapped round the capstan itself). During the raising of an anchor the nippers were attached and detached from the (endless) messenger by the ship's boys. Hence the term for small boys: 'nippers'.
- **No room to swing a cat** – The entire ship's company was expected to witness floggings, assembled on deck. If it was very crowded, the bosun might not have room to swing the 'cat o' nine tails' (the whip).

O

- **Oakum** – Material used for caulking hulls. Often hemp picked from old untwisted ropes.
- **Oilskins** or **oilies** – Foul-weather clothing worn by sailors.
- **Oreboat** – Great Lakes term for a vessel primarily used in the transport of iron ore.
- **Orlop deck** – The lowest deck of a ship of the line. The deck covering in the hold.
- **Outboard motor** – A motor mounted externally on the transom of a small boat. The boat may be steered by twisting the whole motor, instead of or in addition to using a rudder.
- **Outdrive** – The lower part of a sterndrive (*qv*).
- **Outhaul** – A line used to control the shape of a sail.
- **Outward bound** – To leave the safety of port, heading for the open ocean.
- **Overbear** – To sail downwind directly at another ship, stealing the wind from its sails.
- **Overfalls** – Dangerously steep and breaking seas due to opposing currents and wind in a shallow area, or strong currents over a shallow rocky bottom.
- **Overhaul** – Hauling the buntline ropes over the sails to prevent them from chaffing.
- **Overhead** – The "ceiling," or, essentially, the bottom of the deck above you.
- **Over-reaching** – When tacking, holding a course too long.
- **Over the barrel** – Adult sailors were flogged on the back or shoulders while tied to a grating, but boys were beaten instead on the posterior (often bared), with a cane or cat, while bending, often tied down, over the barrel of a gun, known as (kissing) the gunner's daughter.
- **Overwhelmed** – Capsized or foundered.
- **Owner** – traditional Royal Navy term for the Captain, a survival from the days when privately-owned ships were often hired for naval service.

- **Ox-eye** – A cloud or other weather phenomenon that may be indicative of an upcoming storm.

P

- **Panting** – The pulsation in and out of the bow and stern plating as the ship alternately rises and plunges deep into the water
- **Parley** – a discussion or conference, especially between enemies, over terms of a truce or other matters.
- **Parbuckle** – A method of lifting a roughly cylindrical object such as a spar. One end of a rope is made fast above the object, a loop of rope is lowered and passed around the object, which can be raised by hauling on the free end of rope.
- **Parrel** – A movable loop or collar, used to fasten a yard or gaff to its respective mast. Parrel still allows the spar to be raised or lowered and swivel around the mast. Can be made of wire or rope and fitted with beads to reduce friction.
- **Part brass rags** – Fall out with a friend. From the days when cleaning materials were shared between sailors.
- **Paying** – Filling a seam (with caulking or pitch), lubricating the running rigging; paying with slush (q.v.), protecting from the weather by covering with slush. See also: The Devil to pay. (French from *paix*, pitch)
- **Paymaster** – The officer responsible for all money matters in RN ships including the paying and provisioning of the crew, all stores, tools and spare parts. See also: purser.
- **Pennant** – A long, thin triangular flag flown from the masthead of a military ship (as opposed to a burgee, the flags thus flown on yachts).
- **Pier-head jump** – When a sailor is drafted to a warship at the last minute, just before she sails.
- **Pilot** – Navigator. A specially knowledgeable person qualified to navigate a vessel through difficult waters, e.g. harbour pilot etc.
- **PIM** – Points (or plan) of intended movement. The charted course for a naval unit's movements.
- **Pipe (Bos'n's)**, or a **bos'n's call** – A whistle used by Boatswains (bosuns or bos'ns) to issue commands. Consisting of a metal tube which directs the breath over an aperture on the top of a hollow ball to produce high pitched notes. The pitch of the notes can be changed by partly covering the aperture with the finger of the hand in which the pipe is held. The shape of the instrument is similar to that of a smoking pipe.
- **Pipe down** – A signal on the bosun's pipe to signal the end of the day, requiring lights (and smoking pipes) to be extinguished and silence from the crew.
- **Piping the side** – A salute on the bos'n's pipe(s) performed in the company of the deck watch on the starboard side of the quarterdeck or at the head of the gangway, to welcome or bid farewell to the ship's Captain, senior officers and honoured visitors.

- **Pitch** – A vessel's motion, rotating about the beam/transverse axis, causing the fore and aft ends to rise and fall repetitively.
- **Pitchpole** – To capsize a boat stern over bow, rather than by rolling over.
- **Planing** – When a fast-moving vessel skims over the water instead of pushing through it.
- **Pontoon** – A flat-bottomed vessel used as a ferry, barge, car float or a float moored alongside a jetty or a ship to facilitate boarding.
- **Poop deck** – A high deck on the aft superstructure of a ship.
- **Pooped** –
  1. Swamped by a high, following sea.
  2. Exhausted.
- **Port** – Towards the left-hand side of the ship facing forward (formerly Larboard). Denoted with a red light at night.
- **Porthole** or **port** – an opening in a ship's side, esp. a round one for admitting light and air, fitted with thick glass and, often, a hinged metal cover, a window
- **Port tack** – When sailing with the wind coming from the port side of the vessel. Must give way to boats on *starboard tack*.
- **Press gang** – Formed body of personnel from a ship of the Royal Navy (either a ship seeking personnel for its own crew or from a 'press tender' seeking men for a number of ships) that would identify and force (press) men, usually merchant sailors into service on naval ships usually against their will.
- **Preventer** (gybe preventer, jibe preventer) – A sail control line originating at some point on the boom leading to a fixed point on the boat's deck or rail (usually a cleat or pad eye) used to prevent or moderate the effects of an accidental jibe.
- **Privateer** – A privately-owned ship authorised by a national power (by means of a **Letter of marque**) to conduct hostilities against an enemy. Also called a **private man of war**.
- **Propeller walk** or **prop walk** – tendency for a propeller to push the stern sideways. In theory a right hand propeller in reverse will walk the stern to port.
- **Prow** – a poetical alternative term for bows.
- **Purchase** – A mechanical method of increasing force, such as a tackle or lever.
- **Pusser** – Purser, the person who buys, stores and sells all stores on board ships, including victuals, rum and tobacco. Originally a private merchant, latterly a warrant officer.
- **Principal Warfare Officer** – PWO, one of a number of Warfare branch specialist officers.

Q

- **Queen's (King's) Regulations** – The standing orders governing the British Royal Navy issued in the name of the current Monarch.

- **Quarterdeck** – The aftermost deck of a warship. In the age of sail, the quarterdeck was the preserve of the ship's officers.
- **Quayside** – Refers to the dock or platform used to fasten a vessel to

R

- **Rabbet** or **rebate** – A groove cut in wood to form part of a joint.
- **Radar** – Acronym for RAdio Detection And Ranging. An electronic system designed to transmit radio signals and receive reflected images of those signals from a "target" in order to determine the bearing and distance to the "target".
- **Radar reflector** – A special fixture fitted to a vessel or incorporated into the design of certain aids to navigation to enhance their ability to reflect radar energy. In general, these fixtures will materially improve the visibility for use by vessels with radar.
- **Range lights** – Two lights associated to form a range (a line formed by the extension of a line connecting two charted points) which often, but not necessarily, indicates the channel centerline. The front range light is the lower of the two, and nearer to the mariner using the range. The rear light is higher and further from the mariner.
- **Ratlines** – Rope ladders permanently rigged from bulwarks and tops to the mast to enable access to top masts and yards.
- **Reaching** – Sailing across the wind: from about 60° to about 160° off the wind. Reaching consists of "close reaching" (about 60° to 80°), "beam reaching" (about 90°) and "broad reaching" (about 120° to 160°). See also *beating* and *running*.
- **Ready about** – A call to indicate imminent tacking (see *going about*).
- **Receiver of Wreck** – A government official whose duty is to give owners of shipwrecks the opportunity to retrieve their property and ensure that law-abiding finders of wreck receive an appropriate reward.
- **Red Duster** – Traditional nickname for the Red Ensign, the civil ensign (flag) carried by United Kingdom civilian vessels.
- **Reduced cat** – A light version on the cat o'nine tails for use on boys; also called "boys' pussy".
- **Reef**
  1. Reef: To temporarily reduce the area of a sail exposed to the wind, usually to guard against adverse effects of strong wind or to slow the vessel.
  2. Reef: Rock or coral, possibly only revealed at low tide, shallow enough that the vessel will at least touch if not go aground.
- **Reef points** – Small lengths of cord attached to a sail, used to secure the excess fabric after reefing.
- **Reef-bands** – Long pieces of rough canvas sewed across the sails to give them additional strength.
- **Reef-tackles** – Ropes employed in the operation of reefing.

- **Relative bearing** – A bearing relative to the direction of the ship: the clockwise angle between the ship's direction and an object. See also *absolute bearing* and *bearing*.
- **Rigging** – The system of masts and lines on ships and other sailing vessels.
- **Righting couple** – The force which tends to restore a ship to equilibrium once a heel has altered the relationship between her centre of buoyancy and her centre of gravity.
- **Rigol** – The rim or 'eyebrow' above a port-hole or scuttle.
- **Rode** – The anchor line, rope or cable connecting the anchor chain to the vessel. Also Anchor Rode.
- **Roll** – A vessel's motion rotating from side to side, about the fore-aft/longitudinal axis. List (*qv*) is a lasting tilt in the roll direction.
- **Rolling-tackle** – A number of pulleys, engaged to confine the yard to the weather side of the mast; this tackle is much used in a rough sea.
- **The ropes** – the lines in the rigging.
- **Rope's end** – A summary punishment device.
- **Rowlock** – A bracket providing the fulcrum for an oar. Also see *thole*.
- **Rubbing strake** – An extra plank fitted to the outside of the hull, usually at deck level, to protect the topsides.
- **Rummage sale** – A sale of damaged cargo (from French *arrimage*).
- **Running rigging** – Rigging used to manipulate sails, spars, etc. in order to control the movement of the ship. Cf. standing rigging.
- **Running before the wind** or **running** – Sailing more than about 160° away from the wind. If directly away from the wind, it's a *dead run*.

S

- **Sagging** – When the trough of a wave is amidships, causing the hull to deflect so the ends of the keel are higher than the middle. The opposite of hogging.
- **Sail-plan** – A set of drawings showing various sail combinations recommended for use in various situations.
- **Saltie** – Great Lakes term for a vessel that sails the oceans.
- **Sampson post** – A strong vertical post used to support a ship's windlass and the heel of a ship's bowsprit.
- **Scandalize** – To reduce the area and efficiency of a sail by expedient means (slacking the peak and tricing up the tack) without properly reefing, thus slowing boat speed. Also used in the past as a sign of mourning.
- **Scow** –
  1. A method of preparing an anchor for tripping by attaching an anchor cable to the crown and fixing to the ring by a light seizing (also known as becue). The seizing can be broken if the anchor becomes fouled.
  2. A type of clinker dinghy, characteristically beamy and slow.
- **Scud** – A name given by sailors to the lowest clouds, which are mostly observed in squally weather.

- **Scudding** – A term applied to a vessel when carried furiously along by a tempest.
- **Scuppers** – Originally a series of pipes fitted through the ships side from inside the thicker deck waterway to the topside planking to drain water overboard, larger quantities drained through freeing ports, which were openings in the bulwarks.
- **Scuttle** – A small opening, or lid thereof, in a ship's deck or hull.
- **Scuttlebutt** – A barrel with a hole in used to hold water that sailors would drink from. By extension (in modern naval usage), a shipboard drinking fountain or water cooler. Also: gossip.
- **Scuttling** – Cutting a hole in an object or vessel, especially in order to sink a vessel deliberately.
- **Sea anchor** – A stabilizer deployed in the water for heaving to in heavy weather. It acts as a brake and keeps the hull in line with the wind and perpendicular to waves. Often in the form of a large bag made of heavy canvas.
- **Seaboots** – High waterproof boots for use at sea. In leisure sailing, known as *sailing wellies*.
- **Sea chest** – A watertight box built against the hull of the ship communicating with the sea through a grillage, to which valves and piping are attached to allow water in for ballast, engine cooling, and firefighting purposes.
- **Seacock** – a valve in the hull of a boat.
- **Seaman** – Generic term for sailor, or (part of) a low naval rank
- **Seaworthy** – Certified for, and capable of, safely sailing at sea.
- **Self-unloader** – Great Lakes slang term for a vessel with a conveyor or some other method of unloading the cargo without shoreside equipment.
- **Sennet whip** – A summary punitive implement
- **Shakes** – Pieces of barrels or casks broken down to save space. They are worth very little, leading to the phrase "no great shakes".
- **Sheer** – The upward curve of a vessel's longitudinal lines as viewed from the side.
- **Sheer plan** – In shipbuilding, a diagram showing an elevation of the ship's sheer viewed from the broadside.
- **Sheet** – A rope used to control the setting of a sail in relation to the direction of the wind.
- **Sextant** – Navigational instrument used to measure a ship's latitude.
- **Shift tides** – Sighting the positions of the sun and moon using a sextant and using a nautical almanac to determine the location and phase of the moon and calculating the relative effect of the tides on the navigation of the ship.[7][8]
- **Ship** – Strictly, a three-masted vessel square-rigged on all three masts, or on three masts of a vessel with more than three. Hence a ship-rigged barque would be a four master, square-rigged on fore, main and mizzen, with spanker and gaff topsail only on the Jigger-mast. Generally now used to describe most medium or large vessels

146

outfitted with smaller boats. As a consequence of this submarines may be larger than small ships, but are called boats because they do not carry boats of their own.

- **Ship's bell** – Striking the ship's bell is the traditional method of marking time and regulating the crew's watches.
- **Ship's biscuit** – See *hard tack*.
- **Ship's company** – The crew of a ship.
- **Shoal** – Shallow water that is a hazard to navigation.
- **Shoal draught** – Shallow draught, making the vessel capable of sailing in unusually shallow water.
- **Short stay** – A description for the relative slackness of an anchor chain; this term means somewhat slack, but not vertical nor fully extended.
- **Shrouds** – Standing rigging running from a mast to the sides of a ships.
- **Sick bay** – The compartment reserved for medical purposes.
- **Siren** – A sound signal which uses electricity or compressed air to actuate either a disc or a cup shaped rotor.
- **Skeg** – A downward or sternward projection from the keel in front of the rudder. Protects the rudder from damage, and in *bilge keelers* may provide one "leg" of a tripod on which the boat stands when the tide is out.
- **Skipper** – The captain of a ship.
- **Skysail** – A sail set very high, above the royals. Only carried by a few ships.
- **Skyscraper** – A small, triangular sail, above the skysail. Used in light winds on a few ships.
- **Slop chest** – A ship's store of merchandise, such as clothing, tobacco, etc., maintained aboard merchant ships for sale to the crew.
- **Slush** – Greasy substance obtained by boiling or scraping the fat from empty salted meat storage barrels, or the floating fat residue after boiling the crew's meal. In the Royal Navy the perquisite of the cook who could sell it or exchange it (usually for alcohol) with other members of the crew. Used for greasing parts of the running rigging of the ship and therefore valuable to the master and bosun.
- **Slush fund** – The money obtained by the cook selling slush ashore. Used for the benefit of the crew (or the cook).
- **Small bower (anchor)** – The smaller of two anchors carried in the bow.
- **Snow** – A form of brig where the gaff spanker or driver is rigged on a "snow mast" a lighter spar supported in chocks close behind the main-mast.
- **Son of a gun** – The space between the guns was used as a semi-private place for trysts with prostitutes and wives, which sometimes led to birth of children with disputed parentage. Another claim is that the origin the term resulted from firing a ship's guns to hasten a difficult birth.

- **Sonar** – A method of using sound pulses to detect, range and sometime image underwater targets and obstacles, or the bed of the sea. Also see *echo sounding* and *ASDIC*.
- **Sou'wester** -
  1. A storm from the south west.
  2. A type of waterproof hat with a wide brim over the neck, worn in storms.
- **Sounding** – Measuring the depth of the water. Traditionally done by *swinging the lead*, now commonly by echo sounding.
- **Spanker** – A fore-and-aft or gaff-rigged sail on the aft-most mast of a square-rigged vessel and the main fore-and-aft sail (spanker sail) on the aft-most mast of a (partially) fore-and-aft rigged vessel such as a schooner, a barquentine, and a barque.
- **Spanker-mast** – The aft-most mast of a fore-and-aft or gaff-rigged vessel such as schooners, barquentines, and barques. A full-rigged ship has a spanker sail but not a spanker-mast (see Jigger-mast).
- **Spar** – A wooden, in later years also iron or steel pole used to support various pieces of rigging and sails. The big five-masted full-rigged tall ship *Preussen* (German spelling: *Preußen*) had crossed 30 steel yards, but only one wooden spar – the little gaff of its spanker sail.
- **Spindrift** – Finely-divided water swept from crest of waves by strong winds.
- **Spinnaker** – A large sail flown in front of the vessel while heading downwind.
- **Spinnaker pole** – A spar used to help control a spinnaker or other headsail.
- **Spring** – A line used parallel to that of the length of a craft, to prevent fore-aft motion of a boat, when moored or docked.
- **Splice** – To join lines (ropes, cables etc.) by unravelling their ends and intertwining them to form a continuous line. To form an eye or a knot by splicing.
- **Splice the mainbrace** - A euphemism, it is an order given aboard naval vessels to issue the crew with a drink, traditionally grog.
- **Spurling pipe** – A pipe that connects to the chain locker, from which the anchor chain emerges onto the deck at the bow of a ship.
- **Square meal** – A sufficient quantity of food. Meals on board ship were served to the crew on a square wooden plate in harbor or at sea in good weather. Food in the Royal Navy was invariably better or at least in greater quantity than that available to the average landsman. However, while square wooden plates were indeed used on board ship, there is no established link between them and this particular term. The OED gives the earliest reference from the U.S. in the mid 19th century.
- **Squared away** – Yards held rigidly perpendicular to their masts and parallel to the deck. This was rarely the best trim of the yards for efficiency but made a pretty sight for inspections and in harbor. The term is applied to situations and to people figuratively to mean that

all difficulties have been resolved or that the person is performing well and is mentally and physically prepared.

- **Squat effect** is the phenomenon by which a vessel moving quickly through shallow water creates an area of lowered pressure under its keel that reduces the ship's buoyancy, particularly at the bow. The reduced buoyancy causes the ship to "squat" lower in the water than would ordinarily be expected, and thus its effective draught is increased.
- **Stanchion** – vertical post near a deck's edge that supports life-lines. A timber fitted in between the frame heads on a wooden hull or a bracket on a steel vessel, approx one meter high, to support the bulwark plank or plating and the rail.
- **Standing rigging** – Rigging which is used to support masts and spars, and is not normally manipulated during normal operations. Cf. running rigging.
- **Stand-on (vessel)** – A vessel directed to keep her course and speed where two vessels are approaching one another so as to involve a risk of collision.
- **Starboard** – Towards the right-hand side of a vessel facing forward. Denoted with a green light at night. Derived from the old steering oar or *steerboard* which preceded the invention of the rudder.
- **Starboard tack** – When sailing with the wind coming from the starboard side of the vessel. Has right of way over boats on *port tack*.
- **Starter**[disambiguation needed] – A rope used as a punitive device. See teazer, togey.
- **Stay** – Rigging running fore (forestay) and aft (backstay) from a mast to the hull.
- **Staysail** – A sail whose luff is attached to a forestay.
- **Steering flat** – In a vessel, the compartment containing the steering gear.
- **Steering oar** or **steering board** – A long, flat board or oar that went from the stern to well underwater, used to steer vessels before the invention of the rudder. Traditionally on the starboard side of a ship (the "steering board" side).
- **Stem** – The extension of keel at the forward end of a ship.
- **Stern** – The rear part of a ship, technically defined as the area built up over the sternpost, extending upwards from the counter to the taffrail.
- **Stern chaser** – See *chase gun*.
- **Stern tube** – The tube under the hull to bear the tailshaft for propulsion (usually at stern).
- **Sterndrive** – A propeller drive system similar to the lower part of an outboard motor extending below the hull of a larger power boat or yacht, but driven by an engine mounted within the hull. Unlike a fixed propeller (but like an outboard), the boat may be steered by twisting the drive. Also see *inboard motor* and *outboard motor*.
- **Stonnacky** – A punitive device.

- **Stopper knot** – A knot tied in the end of a rope, usually to stop it passing through a hole; most commonly a figure-eight knot.
- **Strake** – One of the overlapping boards in a clinker built hull.
- **Studding-sails** ("stunsail") – Long and narrow sails, used only in fine weather, on the outside of the large square sails.
- **Surge** – A vessel's transient motion in a fore and aft direction.
- **Sway** –
  1. A vessel's lateral motion from side to side.
  2. (v) To hoist: "Sway up my dunnage".
- **Swigging** – To take up the last bit of slack on a line such as a halyard, anchor line or dockline by taking a single turn round a cleat and alternately heaving on the rope above and below the cleat while keeping the tension on the tail.
- **Swinging the compass** – Measuring the accuracy in a ship's magnetic compass so its readings can be adjusted – often by turning the ship and taking bearings on reference points.
- **Swinging the lamp** – Telling sea stories. Referring to lamps slung from the deckhead which swing while at sea. Often used to indicate that the story teller is exaggerating.
- **Swinging the lead** –
  1. Measuring the depth of water beneath a ship using a lead-weighted sounding line. Regarded as a relatively easy job, thus:
  2. Feigning illness etc to avoid a hard job.

T

- **Tabernacle** – A large bracket attached firmly to the deck, to which the foot of the mast is fixed. It has two sides or cheeks and a bolt forming the pivot around which the mast is raised and lowered.
- **Tack** -
  1. A leg of the route of a sailing vessel, particularly in relation to *tacking* (*qv*) and to *starboard tack* and *port tack* (also *qv*).
  2. Hard tack: *qv*.
- **Tacking** -
  1. Zig-zagging so as to sail directly towards the wind (and for some rigs also away from it).
  2. *Going about* (*qv*).
- **Taffrail** – A rail at the stern of the boat that covers the head of the counter timbers.
- **Tailshaft** – A kind of metallic shafting (a rod of metal) to hold the propeller and connected to the power engine. When the tailshaft is moved, the propeller may also be moved for propulsion.
- **Taken aback** – An inattentive helmsmen might allow the dangerous situation to arise where the wind is blowing into the sails 'backwards', causing a sudden (and possibly dangerous) shift in the position of the sails.
- **Taking the wind out of his sails** – To sail in a way that steals the wind from another ship. cf. overbear.

- **Tally** – The operation of hauling aft the **sheets**, or drawing them in the direction of the ship's stern.
- **Teazer** – A rope used as a punitive device.
- **Thole** – Vertical wooden peg or pin inserted through the gunwale to form a fulcrum for oars when rowing. Used in place of a *rowlock*.
- **Three sheets to the wind** – On a three-masted ship, having the sheets of the three lower courses loose will result in the ship meandering aimlessly downwind. Also, a sailor who has drunk strong spirits beyond his capacity.
- **Thwart** – A bench seat across the width of an open boat.
- **Timoneer** – From the French *timonnier*, is a name given, on particular occasions, to the steersman of a ship.
- **Tingle** – A thin temporary patch.
- **Tiller** – a lever used for steering, attached to the top of the rudder post. Used mainly on smaller vessels, such as dinghies and rowing boats.
- **Toe-rail** – A low strip running around the edge of the deck like a low bulwark. It may be shortened or have gaps in it to allow water to flow off the deck.
- **Toe the line** or **Toe the mark** – At parade, sailors and soldiers were required to stand in line, their toes in line with a seam of the deck.
- **Togey** – A rope used as a punitive device
- **Topmast** – The second section of the mast above the deck; formerly the upper mast, later surmounted by the topgallant mast; carrying the topsails.
- **Topgallant** – The mast or sails above the tops.
- **Topsail** – The second sail (counting from the bottom) up a mast. These may be either square sails or fore-and-aft ones, in which case they often "fill in" between the mast and the gaff of the sail below.
- **Topsides** – the part of the hull between the waterline and the deck. Also, Above-water hull
- **Touch and go** – The bottom of the ship touching the bottom, but not grounding.
- **Towing** – The operation of drawing a vessel forward by means of long lines.
- **Travellers** – Small fittings that slide on a rod or line. The most common use is for the inboard end of the mainsheet; a more esoteric form of traveller consists of "slight iron rings, encircling the backstays, which are used for hoisting the top-gallant yards, and confining them to the backstays".
- **Traffic Separation Scheme** – Shipping corridors marked by buoys which separate incoming from outgoing vessels. Improperly called *Sea Lanes*.
- **Transom** – a more or less flat surface across the stern of a vessel. Dinghies tend to have almost vertical transoms, whereas yachts' transoms may be raked forward or aft.
- **Trice** – To haul and tie up by means of a rope.

- **Trick** – A period of time spent at the wheel (*"my trick's over"*).
- **Trim** – Relationship of ship's hull to waterline.
- **True bearing** – An absolute bearing (*qv*) using true north.
- **True north** – The direction of the geographical North Pole.
- **Tumblehome** – A description of hull shape when viewed in a transverse section, where the widest part of the hull is someway below deck level.
- **Turn** – A knot passing behind or around an object.
- **Turnbuckle** – see *bottlescrew*.
- **Turtling** – The condition of a sailboat's (in particular a dinghy's) capsizing to a point where the mast is pointed straight down and the hull is on the surface resembling a turtle shell.

U

- **Unassisted sailing** - A voyage, usually singlehanded, with no intermediate port stops or physical assistance from external sources.
- **Under the weather** – Serving a watch on the weather side of the ship, exposed to wind and spray.
- **Under way** – A vessel that is moving under control: that is, neither at anchor, made fast to the shore, aground nor adrift.
- **Underwater hull** or *underwater ship* – The underwater section of a vessel beneath the waterline, normally not visible except when in drydock.
- **Up-behind** – Slack off quickly and run slack to a belaying point. This order is given when a line or wire has been stopped off or falls have been four-in-hand and the hauling part is to be belayed.
- **Up-and-down** – A description for the relative slackness of an anchor chain; this term means that the anchor chain is slack and hangs vertically down from the hawse pipe.
- **Upper-yardmen** – Specially selected personnel destined for high office.

V

- **Vang**
  1 – A rope leading from gaff to either side of the deck, used to prevent the gaff from sagging.
  2 – See *boom vang*.
- **Vanishing angle** – The maximum degree of heel after which a vessel becomes unable to return to an upright position.
- **V-hull** – The shape of a boat or ship in which the contours of the hull come in a straight line to the keel.

W

- **Wake** – Turbulence behind a vessel. Not to be confused with *wash*.
- **Waist** – the central deck of a ship between the forecastle and the quarterdeck.[9]
- **Wales** – A number of strong and thick planks running length-wise along the ship, covering the lower part of the ship's side.
- **Wash** – The waves created by a vessel. Not to be confused with *wake*.

- **Watch** – A period of time during which a part of the crew is on duty. Changes of watch are marked by strokes on the ship's bell.
- **Watercraft** – Water transport vessels. Ships, boats, personal water craft etc.
- **Waterway**
  1 – Waterway, a navigable body of water.
  2 – A strake of timber laid against the frames or bulwark stanchions at the margin of a laid wooden deck, usually about twice the thickness of the deck planking.
- **Waypoint** – A location defined by navigational coordinates, especially as part of a planned route.
- **Wearing ship** – Tacking away from the wind in a square-rigged vessel. See also *Gybe*.
- **Weather gage** or **weather gauge** – Favorable position over another sailing vessel with respect to the wind.
- **Weather deck** – Whichever deck is that exposed to the weather – usually either the main deck or, in larger vessels, the upper deck.
- **Weather side** – The side of a ship exposed to the wind.
- **Weatherly** – A ship that is easily sailed and maneuvered; makes little leeway when sailing to windward.
- **Weigh anchor** – To heave up (an anchor) preparatory to sailing.
- **Well** – Place in the ship's hold for pumps.
- **White horses** or **whitecaps** – Foam or spray on wave tops caused by stronger winds (usually above Force 4).
- **Wheel** or **ship's wheel** – The usual steering device on larger vessels: a wheel with a horizontal axis, connected by cables to the rudder.
- **Wheelhouse** – Location on a ship where the wheel is located; also called pilothouse or bridge.
- **Whelkie** - A small sailing pram.
- **Wide berth** – To leave room between two ships moored (berthed) to allow space for maneuver.
- **Whipstaff** – A vertical lever connected to a tiller, used for steering on larger ships before the development of the ship's wheel.
- **Windage** – Wind resistance of the boat.
- **Windbound** – A condition wherein the ship is detained in one particular station by contrary winds.
- **Wind-over-tide** – Sea conditions with a tidal current and a wind in opposite directions, leading to short, heavy seas.
- **Windward** – In the direction that the wind is coming from.
- **Windlass** – A winch mechanism, usually with a horizontal axis. Used where mechanical advantage greater than that obtainable by block and tackle was needed (such as raising the anchor on small ships).
- **Worm, serve, and parcel** – To protect a section of rope from chafing by: laying yarns (worming) to fill in the cuntlines, wrapping marline or other small stuff (serving) around it, and stitching a covering of canvas (parceling) over all.

Y

- **Yard** – The horizontal spar from which a square sail is suspended.
- **Yardarm** – The very end of a yard. Often mistaken for a "yard", which refers to the entire spar. As in to hang "from the yardarm" and the sun being "over the yardarm" (late enough to have a drink).
- **Yarr** – Acknowledgement of an order, or agreement. Also *aye, aye*.
- **Yaw** – A vessel's rotational motion about the vertical axis, causing the fore and aft ends to swing from side to side repetitively.

www.ingramcontent.com/pod-product-compliance
Lightning Source LLC
Chambersburg PA
CBHW061135030426

42334CB00003B/51

* 9 7 8 0 9 8 2 9 4 7 7 0 8 *